WEST TEXAS

WEST TEXAS

A Portrait of Its People
and
Their Raw and Wondrous Land

Mike Cochran and John Lumpkin
Foreword by John T. Montford
Photo Editor Ron Heflin

Texas Tech University Press

Design by Tamara Kruciak

Pages ii and iii: A lone willow on the plain near Benjamin. Photo by Wyman Meinzer.

Printed in Hong Kong

Library of Congress Cataloging-in-Publication Data
    Cochran, Mike.
        West Texas : a portrait of its people and their
    raw and wondrous land / Mike Cochran and
    John Lumpkin ; foreword by John T. Montford.
            p. cm.
        ISBN 0-89672-426-3 (alk. paper)
        1. Texas, West—History. 2. Texas, West
    Anecdotes. 3. Texas, West—Description and
    travel. I. Lumpkin, John. II. Title.
    F386.C645 1999
    976.4—dc21   99-36542
                                  CIP

00 01 02 03 04 05 06 07 / 9 8 7 6 5 4 3

Texas Tech University Press
Box 41037
Lubbock, Texas 79409-1037 USA

800-832-4042

ttup@ttu.edu

Http://www.ttup.ttu.edu

Foreword

Sometimes I think I've approached life backwards.

When I was growing up, it seemed as if the migration in Texas was from west to east. Everybody living west of Interstate 35 was in a hurry to move east of Interstate 35. They were leaving small to medium-sized communities and moving to the big cities in the center of the state.

I grew up in the mid-cities area of Dallas and Fort Worth and attended law school in Austin. When I earned my degree, completed my military service in the Marine Corps, and looked for a place to practice, I went against the grain. I moved east to west and settled down in the heart of West Texas—Lubbock.

Like so many other young people just starting out, my first job was only a stopping point in my career. But, you know, West Texas grows on you. And it grows on you quickly.

I've called myself a West Texan ever since I moved here. And today, West Texas is still my home. It always will be.

What can be said about a place as special as West Texas? To be honest, it's really hard to define as a region. Fort Worth calls itself the City Where the West Begins. People as far south as Brady also call themselves West Texans. People as far north as Wichita Falls consider themselves residents of West Texas.

As you'll read in this book, West Texas is all the cities and towns mentioned above and a whole lot more. I'll let the authors take the responsibility of saying where it begins and where it ends. I'm afraid I'd leave something out.

West Texas is an open, friendly place with a whole lot of open, friendly people. Almost everything about West Texas is honest. When you move out here, you can look at the package and know what you're getting. Of course, then you realize you are getting a whole lot more than you bargained for.

As a young lawyer, I joined one of Lubbock's finest law firms. The firm had mostly civil lawyers, with a client list of some of the region's most prominent business people. I, on the other hand, was the token criminal defense lawyer. It's safe to say that my clients made the firm a little nervous. It was not unusual to walk in and see an accused safe cracker sitting in the firm's waiting room along with a bank president. During the savings and loan crisis, you couldn't tell one from the other. I started to sense the firm's uneasiness when the receptionist began asking my clients to leave via the back door.

To build my practice and learn about the entire region, I started traveling the area defending clients. There were circuit judges who went from county to county hearing cases. I went from county to county representing clients.

That experience sold me on West Texas. I got to know hundreds of people because I tried so many jury cases. In small towns, I visited coffee shops, co-ops, and courthouses. I drove along the open highways. West Texas grabbed a hold of me and I don't think it will ever let go.

The land is open and the sky is blue. There is not a sunset or sunrise anywhere in the United States that compares with those in West Texas. The vanishing point in the horizon constantly positions itself in the center of your windshield or in your rearview mirror. West Texans are blessed with natural resources: oil, rich farm land, a good climate, and enough water to let us get by. But West Texas is not easy. You have to work for what you get.

In West Texas, you never feel confined. Every drive is an experience. When you go out to eat or stop for a cup of coffee, you see people who represent a cross section of life. There are farmers and businessmen, oil barons and roughnecks, and doctors and college professors.

The people are tough and gritty. That is because they have had to do things the hard way. They have seen boom days and busts in the oil fields. They have seen years when cotton and other crops were abundant. And they have seen years when droughts have left their land barren. But they never give up. The people of West Texas live by the credo that tomorrow will be a better day.

Most days it is. Ask the citizens of Roby. Locked in a drought one year, the farming community was struggling when forty-three of its citizens went in together and bought lottery tickets. The group won almost fifty million dollars and the whole town benefited. In fact, it was rescued from oblivion.

West Texans don't think they are special, but I think we accept that we are unique. We certainly don't think we are better than anybody else is, but we sure know we are every bit as good. (You know, it really isn't too late to consider statehood.)

My trips through West Texas helped me learn a lot about the region and they also helped me build a political base. I was elected Criminal District Attorney for Lubbock County in 1978 and later to the Texas Senate. My Senate district stretched from Lubbock to San Angelo and all the way to El Paso.

The people in my district were loyal. They never expected me to do anything but believe them. They just wanted their due. Their requests were simple—good roads, good schools, access to good health care, and a whole lot less government.

I continued to travel my circuit after I was elected senator and still travel it today as Chancellor of Texas Tech University and Health Sciences Center. I can't get enough of the land or the people.

As you will discover in this book, there are no better storytellers than people in West Texas. As I said, West Texans are good people, but they do have a little wild streak. And they are a whole lot of fun.

When I campaigned, I would regularly stop at a certain co-op to have coffee. It was the best coffee I have ever had. It was also the place to hear from the big thinkers of that town. Once, the coffeepot ran dry and I volunteered to make more. When I looked in the large metal pot, I saw a rusty bolt at the bottom. I left it there, but later mentioned it to one of the regulars. He said it had been there for years. Of course, I should have known. The rusty bolt is what made the coffee so good and it also provided a little iron supplement for those in attendance.

In my travels in this vast land, I also learned there was a shortage of rest stops. Texas Tech students going home to Dallas or Fort Worth or Wichita Falls didn't have anyplace to stop for a restroom except at the sandstone ones behind the Texaco in Guthrie. I lobbied my colleagues in the state Senate and prodded the Texas Department of Transportation so people traveling in West Texas would have a place to stop halfway between Lubbock and the Dallas-Fort Worth metroplex. After years of cajoling, a public rest stop was built.

While I was driving one day from a lake near Fort Worth, a new crudely crafted sign outside the rest stop near Benjamin caught my eye. The sign announced the Senator John T. Montford Memorial Potty. I nearly had a wreck. Highway officials had hurriedly erected the sign as a joke. In fact, they left in such a hurry that a hammer was still lying on the ground in a picture taken of the sign.

Trail rides are a permanent fixture in West Texas, and sometimes the cow ponies are not all that tame. One year, some of my colleagues in the state Senate and some other elected officials participated in such an event.

We camped at the edge of Caprock Canyon in Briscoe County. There was a real campfire and bedrolls, just like in an old cow camp. A heavy frost covered the ground at dawn. The horses were frisky and a little green. When then state Senator John Sharp tried to crawl aboard, his horse started bucking before Sharp hit the saddle. The horse bucked right through the campfire, knocking a quickly emptying coffeepot into the gloom. Finally, after horse and rider disappeared into the dawn, Lieutenant Governor Bill Hobby, an excellent horseman, rode out to calm Sharp's mount and lead both back.

When the laughter stopped, Senator Bob Glasgow of Stephenville swung into his saddle and was promptly bucked, barely missing a patch of cactus. Neither of these gentlemen

School bus near Ropesville in Hockley County, early 1900s

was injured and we soon were able to begin our descent into one of West Texas's grand sights—Caprock Canyon. Like I said, such rewards are earned when you are in West Texas.

Once I was recovering from a broken back sustained in a car accident when the lively mayor of Littlefield dropped by the hospital. He had smuggled in a thermos full of whiskey that looked as big as a fire hydrant. We had cocktails right in the hospital. He even brought two glasses. Now that's what amounts to a touch of West Texas class.

I think this book by Mike Cochran and John Lumpkin will tell you a lot about West Texas. The pictures and stories in this book are a part of West Texas's grand heritage. Read and enjoy. I'm sure West Texas will grow on any of you who aren't from our region just as it has those of us lucky enough to call West Texas home.

John T. Montford
Chancellor
Texas Tech University and
Health Sciences Center

For Sondra, a good ol' Stamford girl,
And for all the guys and gals
Who make West Texas such a literary adventure.
—M. C.

For Eileen, Robin and John, Jim and Lorene,
And the memories of Dad and Ponder Elene.
—J. L.

Where Is West Texas?

Where is our West Texas?

Start with the obvious—it's west of East. That fixes it west of Interstate 35, Texas's Main Street. Although I-35 passes through a town called West near Waco, our West Texas is west of that, but only slightly.

"West" may be Fort Worth—Amon Carter said so—but Dallas is not. Some argue that West Texas begins at the Brazos west of Fort Worth, but that great river angles southeast before West Texas's southern boundaries are set.

The West Texas Chamber of Commerce, no longer in business, once appropriated Kerrville in the Texas Hill Country. Even if that's a stretch, there are big ranches and also a town called Grit on the Hill Country's western borders that must be included. Not too far away stands old Fort McKavett, an early base for West Texas explorer Colonel Ranald Mackenzie.

Is Del Rio too far south? Perhaps, but it's farther west than Abilene and even San Angelo.

Here is our West Texas—a definition based more on eyesight and experience than academic research, more from intuition instead of intellect.

Locate the uncluttered western horizon, the treeless plain. Go where the land prefers mesquite and thistle rather than pine. Where there are no twenty-four-hour traffic jams. Where there are no downtowns with dozens of soaring glass boxes that block the sun at dawn and dusk. Find a place that yields only to those who persevere.

Then draw a line around it. The line would move north from Fort Worth on a slightly western tack, striking the Red River just east of Wichita Falls. It would include the Texas Panhandle; otherwise, how could West Texas claim legendary trail driver Charles Goodnight?

Where the Panhandle ends, the Texas South Plains begin and that incorporates Lubbock. Farther south is the Permian Basin and its gigantic pool of oil. The line moves west along the Texas–New Mexico border all the way to El Paso; if not, why did they once call El Paso's state university Texas Western?

Author A. C. Greene, a native of Abilene, had a very personal boundary for West Texas in his book, *A Personal Country*. It was generally west of the Brazos, south of the Red River, north of San Saba, and east of the Caprock. It stopped at the Pecos River.

But the landscape changed not at all for the cowboys and cattle that once waded across the Pecos, and that's the same today for pickups and semitractor trailers that scoot over the tiny river's bridges.

To us, west of the Pecos is still "West," the West of *Giant* and the West of Big Bend, a vast region formed by the sweeping turn in the Rio Grande as it flows out of Texas's rocky and rugged mountains toward the sea.

If the Red forms the northern boundary, the Rio Grande is natural for the south, all the way to the mouth of the Pecos above Del Rio. From there, take the line northeastward along the Hill Country border up to Fort Worth and you're done.

M. C. and J. L.
Fort Worth, Texas
1 June 1999

Horse grazing in the late evening

"The sunups and sunsets will bring a fainting spell to you."

Hallie Stillwell, owner of the Stillwell Ranch, 1991

A soaptree yucca on a hill near Orla in far West Texas

The big coffee-table picture books of recent years, though, don't come close. They show no pictures of my province or even of neighboring provinces. They leave a big hole in Texas.

James Corder, *Lost in West Texas,* 1988

1

West Texas is a red sunrise in the Palo Duro Canyon, a blustery whitecap Sunday on Lake Meredith, and a purple sunset in the Chisos Mountains of the Big Bend National Park.

It is a whirling windmill west of Amarillo, embracing the Panhandle's most plentiful resource, the wind. Or maybe just hawks circling silently above the Pecos River Gorge near Amistad.

It's St. Patrick's Day in Shamrock, the Fourth of July at the Texas Cowboy Reunion in Stamford, and the Cowboy Christmas Ball in Anson.

West Texas is a South Plains duster, a Sanderson flood, a High Plains hail storm, and everywhere a target for killer heat waves and relentless dry spells. Or being stranded on I-40 in an Amarillo blizzard.

It's Hank the Cowdog, Ace Reid's cowboy cartoons, Joe Allen's ribeyes, and the abandoned shell of a drive-in theater with its crumbling marquee: *Gone With the Wind.*

It's a monument to a mule at Muleshoe, a jackrabbit statue at Odessa, and an eleven-foot tall roadrunner named Paisano Pete at Fort Stockton.

It is the XIT, the SMS, the 6666, the Waggoner, and all the vast ranching empires with their enchanting myths and legends and stories, some of them actually true.

West Texas is oil boom and oil bust and countless oil pumps nodding like stoic insects in a monotonous prairie ritual.

It is the shards of darkness and light in the fifteen-hundred-foot depth of Big Bend's Santa Elena Canyon and the sound of distant thunder in the Double Mountains. Or simply the view from a barren hill near Boys Ranch where the cottonwoods shimmer in the Canadian River valley below.

It's Fort Davis, Fort Concho, Fort Stockton, Fort Phantom Hill, and any number of desolate outposts where troops gathered to protect settlers from the perils of the frontier.

It is the massive shuttered Baker Hotel in Mineral Wells, which is too expensive to redevelop or even implode.

It's also an abandoned airplane hanger at Pyote, where World War II pilots trained and the Enola Gay once flew. For obvious reasons, they called it "The Rattlesnake Bomber Base."

Lone mountain rises above the desert landscape in Brewster County, Big Bend

It is the wonder of sheepdogs on a rock-strewn ranch near Robert Lee and golf courses where pump jacks loom as unnatural hazards. It's prairie dogs, prairie grass, and prairie fires. Mule deer in a thicket near Christoval and pheasant in the corn stubble near Plainview. Wild turkey in the Hill Country and javelina near Comstock. The pronghorn at Alpine and the diamondback rattler near Sweetwater.

West Texas is singing "America the Beautiful" at a Rotary Club luncheon in Childress,

really the first day of the next drought. Or re-tired school teacher Ila Johnston, 93, of Spur, who said, "Life keeps me hippety-hopping."

It's a waitress at the Dairy Queen in Paducah, who says things could be worse, but adds, "If you worry about not having shoes, you'll find somebody without feet."

Or the South Plains legislator who once said, "Don't waste a good man by sending him to Austin . . . Send me; I'm already ruined."

It's a sheriff in Tahoka named Booger Redwine and a high school football coach in Lubbock named Goober Keyes. Speaking of football, it's not the malicious coach played by Jon Voight in the 1999 movie *Varsity Blues* but the gentle drawl of Texas Tech's real-life Spike Dykes, who led the Red Raiders to four consecutive bowls in the same decade.

It's little towns with no stoplights, but ablaze with lights ringing the rodeo arena. Or, it's petro-rich Midland, with its aptly named downtown thoroughfare, Wall Street.

It's Quanah's Medicine Mounds, four mysterious, cone-shaped hills where Coman-ches believed potent spirits dwelled. The town is named for the Comanches' last great chief, Quanah Parker, whose ancestors ruled the West Texas prairie for thousands of years.

It's descending from the Caprock near Post at sundown as the shadows engulf the craggy hills, the scrub oak, and the sagebrush and the lights flicker on atop the oil rigs sprinkled across the plains.

Or leaving the state's only mountain trout stream and stumbling into the shifting, wind-sculptured sand dunes, called the Texas Sahara but in fact is Monahans Sandhills State Park.

It's seeing Wichita Falls darkened and devastated by a killer tornado in 1979 and recalling a similar sickening sight at day-break in Lubbock ten years earlier.

It's the wind-driven dirt that blinds mo-torists along Interstate 20 between Fort Worth and El Paso. But it is also the farmland thick with cotton, wheat, corn, and onions

then blessing the Lord for bringing the rain and praising the senior citizens for bringing the food.

Or maybe it's fictional Tuna, the most West Texas of towns, which exists only on a theater marquee.

Or Caput, which really is.

Elsewhere, it's the realism of a wheat farmer who believed the day after it rains is

3

bursting from the fertile soil atop the Ogallala Aquifer, a subterranean miracle that may be doomed to run dry some day.

It's Dumas, who's proud of its Ding Dong Daddies, or Odessa, which flirted with the slogan, "Odessa is Crude."

It's the echo of a Roaring Twenties orchestra at the Settles Hotel in Big Spring and the memory of tuxedoes and top hats that led Will Rogers to say, "They just don't throw parties the ways they used to at the Settles."

It's now a beer bust on the Concho River and a drug bust on the Rio Grande. A chili cook-off in Terlingua, a Lamb Blast in San Angelo. It's longhorns and longnecks, Friday night football and Saturday night fever.

West Texas is nightfall in the Franklin Mountains, overlooking the low-rise sprawl of El Paso, a city of charm and style, and the allure of Juarez, whose rugged features blur and soften once the sun is gone.

It's not enough rain, too many tornadoes, and just the right amount of twang and economy of speech to drive a carpetbagger over the edge.

It's needing money so bad that towns compete for the nation's hazardous wastes, along with a booster who said, "They've got to educate people that they're not going to glow in the dark."

It is a wary and weary sense of humor that would move a San Angelo resident named Mike Williams to compare the taste of his West Texas water supply to "a gallon of water off the coast of Key West, strained through a leaky asbestos roof into an Appalachian coal miner's bathtub, dumped over his floor and into a tin can formerly used as a silkworm farm and currently in the back alley of Sunset Boulevard." Then, said Mike, it's "aged for five years in a rusty culvert under a deserted highway in Brazil, then buried

A narrow gorge in Caprock Canyons State Park near Quitaque

4

Blooms on a West Texas prickly pear

in William Perry's oldest shoes under a toxic waste dump for a week, put in a beer bottle found in the cellar after ten years and set adrift in the Pacific Ocean until found floating in the swamps of Vietnam, carried in the sun over the Himalayas by a marathon runner until it reaches Europe." For good measure, it is "once again set adrift in the ocean and, after the currents carry the bottle through the jungles of South America, it is put on the back of a tortoise traveling through the Mexican desert to San Angelo, where it is put in the pipes running through the sewers and a sludge pit straight to your tap."

In sum, West Texas is a blend of western fact and fiction, the Old West and the New West, a vast and diverse and wide open land, sometimes very private and almost always too personal.

It is the good and bad that one comes to expect in a large and lusty state with a history of violence and a legacy of crude oil and crude people. People purportedly with too much money or not enough, too much power or none at all. Too little patience and only an occasional trace of humility. But a place that is almost always too generous and often too self-conscious.

All of which makes West Texas raw and wondrous and mean and marvelous and totally splendid misery.

Rolling prairie land east of the Caprock

Wildflowers in Monahans Sandhills State Park

A German artist named Ludwig Bemelmans once visited far West Texas, exploring its forbidding but majestic mountains. Afterwards he said, "It is what Beethoven reached for in music. It will make you breathe deeply whenever you think of it, for you have inhaled eternity."

Let a man travel six weeks in western Texas; and if he is not cured . . . of whatever ailment he has, it will be because there is no blood left in him.

Texas Almanac, 1873

Diners at the Brownwood Country Club glanced up from their salad and sirloin one Saturday night to see gun-toting strangers descending on the kitchen. Moments later, a waitress emerged, looking a mite sheepish.

"I don't think we're going to serve you all anything else," she whispered. "Everyone in the kitchen has their hands up." Invading drug agents soon left with their target, the chef, in tow.

And so it goes in West Texas, zany and unpredictable, often maligned, ill-defined, and misunderstood. It is a place where folks considered bootlegging not a crime but a public service. Where a guy could lose a million dollars and laugh about it. Where a rookie roughneck might find himself welcomed to the oil business with a rattlesnake on the floorboard of his truck. Where a judge once ruled with an iron fist and a tipsy bear.

It is a geographical misnomer. If Fort Worth is truly the City Where the West Begins, then most of the state somehow lies in West Texas. More than a state of mind, it is a world unto itself—and fiercely proud of it. John Steinbeck would understand how it is that the center of the universe lies on a remote West Texas ranch surrounded by cows and guarded by mountain lions and mesquite. "Like most passionate nations," he wrote in *Travels With Charley,* "Texas has its own history based on, but not limited by, facts."

Because most Texans agree that their state is the core of the cosmos, Lone Star logic dictates that the centers of Texas and the universe are therefore one and the same. That's why the center of the universe—as well as the center of Texas—is twenty miles northeast of Brady in McColloch County. An official historical marker says so. It's across a rusty cattle guard, down a gravel road, up a rocky cow trail, past two grazing deer, and atop a ridge decorated with cedar trees and a scattering of cactus.

All this makes Brady's West Texas heritage questionable, at best. But, by necessity, West Texans make the most of what they've got, or maybe even wish they had. That may explain why you find a statue of Alley Oop's dinosaur in Iraan, a bronze of Peter Pan in Mary Martin's Weatherford, and an art gallery with a Picasso at the old jailhouse in Albany.

There is a monument in the town of Panhandle to the first tree planted beyond the Caprock. It's dead now, the victim of a chemical overdose. In Monahans, there is a

The storied Settles Hotel in Big Spring

museum in an oil storage tank, and in nearby Wickett, the traveling Roadkill Café. Says Roadkill's chef: "You kill it—We grill it."

Dalhart was first called "Twist," then "Denrock." Just beyond the downtown railroad underpass is a marker topped by an empty saddle—a widow's tribute to an XIT cowboy. The best grave marker in all of Texas may be the guitar on Buddy Holly's gravestone in Lubbock. They honor the memory of Bonanza's Hoss Cartwright in tiny O'Donnell where Dan Blocker grew up.

Not far from Amarillo, on Interstate 40, a fellow named Steve Thomas erected a 190-foot metal cross as an "advertisement for Jesus." Said he: "We see all sorts of advertising for Satan. Why aren't we seeing any done for Jesus?"

Meanwhile, there was a guy near Abilene who every other year or so rolled his Lincoln out of the garage and into an approaching hailstorm. Why? An insurance scam.

A wealthy rancher convicted of smuggling drugs arrived as ordered at the federal prison in Big Spring. In his private jet.

Although Texas Christian's Horned Frogs may disagree, the most famous horny toad (a misnomer—it's actually a lizard) of all was Old Rip, who was sealed in a cornerstone of a courthouse in Eastland in 1897. To this day, Eastlanders swear Old Rip was found alive and kicking when the courthouse was replaced in 1928. He's now on display in the courthouse in a glass casket. Dead, they say.

A modern-day poker game in Odessa erupted in gunfire. The lone survivor fled to a nearby house for help . . . and was shot to death by the frightened occupant.

A West Texas district attorney advised the local newspaper publisher that there was a bookie operation in his newsroom. "Perfect cover," said the surprised publisher. "Lot of phone calls going in and out all night."

The little Panhandle town of Lefors once tried to give itself away, offering fourteen free residential lots in a drawing. Only four winners came forward. Worse, confessed the city secretary, "I haven't heard from those people in quite some time." The city of Graham, near Possum Kingdom Lake, once posted five-thousand-dollar rewards for anyone who could lure new business or industry to town. It got some quick hits, but not all were welcome. "There's been a lot of inquiries about a cathouse for Graham, but that doesn't qualify," said a grinning city official.

Burkburnett was less choosy, and the rowdy shenanigans surrounding that city's oil boom inspired the 1941 Clark Gable–Spencer Tracy movie *Boomtown*.

Thurber, site of an early brick-making plant, was one of the world's first all-electric cities and home to ten thousand souls. It survives as an exit on Interstate 20 with a restaurant and a population of eight.

The fifteen-story Settles Hotel in Big Spring is an eyesore no more. It was much too big to tear down, so donors simply encased the empty structure with modern windows instead.

A day after Governor George W. Bush declared an emergency because of the 1999 drought, Lubbock was pounded by rain. Cotton farmer R. L. Wyatt exclaimed: "He definitely has my vote."

When a meteor crater was belatedly discovered near Odessa, promoters sealed off the site to make it a tourist attraction. Neighborhood kids found another, smaller meteor in Monahans, but the city council confiscated it because of lucrative offers for the rock. After the kids appeared on national TV, the council gave it back. A guy eventually paid

the kids twenty-three thousand dollars for the soccer ball-sized treasure and everybody went away happy.

By the way, there is a town called Happy in the Panhandle. It's known as "The Little Town Without a Frown."

First-time visitors to Seymour could be in for a mild shock. Once a year, folks padlock just about every business in town, hang out a Gone Fishing sign and head en masse to a nearby lake. And there they spend the weekend chasing the wily bass.

The Unabomber's brother, David Kaczynski, once took refuge in a small cabin in the desert surrounding Big Bend. Like Ted, he was more than a little reclusive, but acquaintances say David also was sociable and

Paisano Pete, who stands at the corner of U.S. 290 and Main Street in Fort Stockton, may be the world's largest roadrunner.

Statue in Ballinger honors a local cowboy, Charles Noyes, who was killed in a range accident.

amiable when he surfaced from time to time with his wife Linda.

Stealing a page from a popular restaurant chain, a couple of entrepreneurs triggered a mighty uproar in the Bible Belt city of Abilene when they opened a bar and grill called Knockers. It was a hoot, so to speak, but short-lived. The cops soon arrested the owners for theft, chased off the comely waitresses, and padlocked the joint.

Speaking of joints, there's a fried chicken palace in Sweetwater like none other. It's called Allen's, and a typical all-you-can-eat seven-dollar lunch includes heaping bowls of red beans, green beans, hominy, creamed corn, squash, okra gumbo, sweet potatoes, sliced buttered potatoes, potato salad, pea salad, and cole slaw. Not to mention iced tea, hot rolls, roast beef, cream gravy, and peach cobbler.

And the chicken? The book *Road Food* describes it thusly: "It is sheathed in a lovely, crackling-crisp crust, juicy and loaded with flavor inside, a perfect blend of spice, crunch, juice, and balmy bird flavor."

The only thing missing is cornbread. "We don't get up early enough to do that anymore," said Billy Allen, whose grandmother Lizzie fried the first bird in 1952.

One unusually dry spring, the city of San Angelo's backup water source was so awful tasting that it inspired a "Describe the Water Contest" by local newspaper columnist Jack Cowan. Yvonne Carter's winning entry: "San Angelo water tastes like it's been filtered through the dust and drippings scraped off a Trashaway sanitation truck with a sweaty palm during its final trip to the dump grounds on a sweltering summer day with a

Yesica Garcia, left, and Claudia Garcia (unrelated) comprised the entire graduating class of Big Bend High School in Study Butte, 1998. This was said to be the smallest graduating class in the state.

load of chumming fish and dead minnows from Eddie's Bait Shop."

In Anson, cafe owner Jack Hornsby routinely left his doors unlocked at night so customers could drift by to make a pot of coffee or a sandwich. Besides, he said, he didn't want burglars busting down his doors.

An Amarillo judge once ordered a bilingual Hispanic woman to speak English to her five-year-old daughter, maintaining that the child's ignorance of English was abusive and doomed her to life as a maid. He later rescinded the order and apologized.

Abilene observed its one-hundredth birthday in 1981 by erecting a model of a drilling rig at the fairgrounds. Unintentionally, oil was discovered.

Wichita Falls spent a hundred thousand dollars for an abstract statue of its official symbol, a crape myrtle. With the city in an uproar, a prankster erected a sign prohibiting laughter during certain hours. There were no water falls in Wichita Falls until boosters paid almost a half million dollars to create one along U.S. 287. Then they threw a party for the faux falls, calling it the "Biggest Turn-on in Texas."

Modern-day Big Spring would not have a spring without a pump.

San Angelo's civic charms include Miss Hattie's Museum, a bright-red, richly restored bordello.

There are ancient pictographs at Hueco Tanks near El Paso, at Paint Rock near San Angelo and along the Rio Grande near Langtry. Just who painted them and why is a secret that is ten thousand years old.

The first West Texans of European descent were the Spanish conquistadors, though their legacy was dubious. Vasquez de Coronado entered the Llano Estacado by way of New Mexico in 1541. Tricked by a Pawnee guide into believing there was an empire named Quivera, he needed a compass to negotiate the plain and apparently wandered into what is now Kansas.

Cisco housed the first hotel to bear Conrad Hilton's name. The legendary innkeeper rented rooms in eight-hour shifts during an oil boom.

One year, the graduating class at remote Big Bend High School numbered a grand total of two.

The mayor of a small West Texas town once fired the cops, who sued the mayor, who was ousted by the city council, which resigned to protest the cop firing. Got that? A cop shot a guy, who sued the city, which fired the cop, who brought criminal charges against the mayor, who fired the judge, who sued the mayor. Uh huh. Then there was the

Remains of Fort Phantom Hill near Abilene. Established in 1851, abandoned in 1854

related bomb threat at the Rinky Dink Cafe and the siege of city hall, which prompted the ousted cops to deputize their buddies to guard a meeting that the mayor insisted was illegal. It all happened in 1983 at Tye, population twenty-two hundred, where the townspeople complained that the folks in nearby Abilene seldom visited except to loot stores, vandalize trailer parks, dump bodies, and put the finishing touches on weekend drinking binges. By the way, the Tye mayor was named Jim Snowden, but they called him Hitler and claimed he ruled the town like a dictator. Sniffed Mayor Jim: "I wish I was a dictator. It would be the most efficient government we could have."

There was no government in the Big Bend ghost town of Terlingua when humorist Wick Fowler decided to stage a chili cook-off in 1967. No matter. People still come from hundreds of miles to pour cold beer and hot chili down their sun-reddened necks.

When it comes to celebrations, all Texans are a bit crazy, and West Texans a little more so. Where else but Texas would you find a Possum Fair, a Mule Day, a Crappiethon, a Rocky Mountain Oyster Fry, a Shrimporee, a Hushpuppy Olympics, a Spam-o-Rama, or Olney's One Arm Dove Hunt? Who but Texans would assemble for onion, oatmeal, corn, peanut, sausage, kolache, strawberry,

Lights of the Rio Grande's twin cities of El Paso and Juarez

rice, black-eyed pea, mosquito, boll weevil, and fire ant festivals?

Texans toss cow chips, round up rattlesnakes and race horses, dogs, cars, turkeys, and armadillos year after year. They raft, rope, ride, sing, fling, dance, fiddle, lie, shoot, fish, hunt, drink, and eat in the name of fun, history, tradition, legend, myth, or whatever strikes the local fancy.

And then there's football. Odessa Permian's football dynasty of the 1980s was so captivating that its high school teams drew larger crowds than some major colleges and inspired a best-selling book, *Friday Night Lights.* The 1990s were less kind: Permian lost to cross-town Odessa High for the first time in three decades.

During a football game at Lubbock, host Texas Tech was penalized because zealous fans insisted on throwing tortillas on the

Brownwood pawnshop manager Keith Neal

Traditional dancers at the West Texas Native American POWWOW, Lubbock

field. In another tortilla toss at Texas Tech, thirty-five thousand fans gathered in Jones Stadium in 1993 to welcome home the Lady Raiders, the women's basketball team that had just won the university's first national championship. When superstar forward Sheryl Swoopes was introduced, teammates and coaches dropped to their knees and bowed. "We kicked butts and took names," said a smiling Swoopes.

In 1856, writing in *Expedition Through Unexplored Texas,* W. B. Parker assessed West Texas thusly: "For all purposes of human habitation—except it might be for a penal colony—these wilds are totally unfit." Today, author A. C. Greene insists West Texas is, as he named his book, *A Personal Country,* a vast mix of conflicts and contradictions scattered throughout large, small, and remote cities, mountains, prairies, deserts, ranchlands, and farmlands. Its people are fiercely independent and universally tough, earthy, plain, and proud.

Lighthouse Rock, Palo Duro Canyon, in the Texas Panhandle

A wordsmith named George Autry said God was working on West Texas when darkness fell, delaying his plans to include such wonders as lakes and trees. By daybreak, the ground had hardened "like concrete." God's solution, said Autry: "I'll just make some people who like it this way."

A lot of people like El Paso. The state's westernmost city, it is also the largest in West Texas with a population in 1998 of nearly six hundred thousand. Flanked by mile-high peaks and nestled in an ancient mountain pass from which it derives its name, El Paso is about as close to Los Angeles as it is to Houston. In fact, it's not even in the same time zone with the rest of the state. It is, however, one of only a handful of the nation's cities where folks can stroll out their back door, cross a river, and watch a bullfight in Mexico.

To the northeast is the High Plains, a windswept land alternately barren and blessed, depending in part on the erratic flow of underground water. Where the soil is fertile, or at least exposed to water, there is corn, wheat, milo, maize, sorghum, soybeans, sunflowers, and King Cotton.

The region's most enduring treasure is Palo Duro Canyon, where a golden sunset reflects off the reddish and rocky walls,

The Girvin Social Club, west of the Pecos River between McCamey and Fort Stockton, 1998. The establishment is in the "new" town of Girvin on U.S. 67, after the town was moved there in the 1950s. Girvin was once a railhead for shipping cattle.

Abandoned corral, Caprock Canyons State Park

spires, and pinnacles. It is nothing less than spiritual. Considered Texas's own little "Grand Canyon," the Palo Duro encompasses 16,402 acres and is ninety million years old.

Less fetching is a chunk of land about halfway between Dallas and Lubbock christened "The Big Empty" by native son Jim Corder, late author of a whimsical reminiscence entitled *Lost in West Texas.* Larger than a couple of New England states combined, it has fewer than twenty-five thousand people, many living on small farms and ranches.

"My part of West Texas doesn't show up much in books," wrote Corder, who, like most West Texans, found a special comeliness where sometimes little exists. His inspiration was the mesquite, the cactus, the tumbleweeds, the red and rocky terrain, and the purple and gray stunted hills.

Outsiders, he said, miss the strange and lonesome beauty such as "the view one sees of the Double Mountains down the Salt Fork from the highway bridge between Swenson and Jayton; the first dramatic drop into the deep of the Croton Breaks . . . ." They also miss the rural majesty of Old Glory fluttering above the tiny post office in Old Glory and the small-town rivalry of six-man football games between such teams as the Rochester Steers and Jayton Jaybirds.

With no special identity such as the Texas Hill Country or the Piney Woods or the Gulf Coast, the Big Empty is often overlooked or ignored even by other Texans. In 1998, *Texas Highways* magazine published the results of reader polls listing the top scenic views, best restaurants, best historic sites, most beautiful buildings, top tourist sites, and so forth. The Big Empty and the Big Country that

West Texas geometry—fields watered by circle irrigation

embraces most of it got short shrift, much to the chagrin of the natives. One, Ken Ellsworth of Abilene, responded in the pages of the *Abilene Reporter-News.* "Have they never driven into Albany from the west and looked down from the hill at the gleaming courthouse that looks like a diamond floating in an emerald, leafy sea?" he asked suspiciously. "Have they never driven past Abilene State Park headed toward Coronado's Camp on U.S. Hwy. 277 in the fall and seen the brilliant oaks mixed with the green of cedar and the autumn colors drifting on and rippling on the clear waters of Elm Creek as it winds its way toward Lake Abilene?"

Nope, he concluded.

"Or," he continued, "have they ever looked with wonder at the twin peaks of the Double Mountains in northern Fisher County that look like two incredibly ragged humps on a camel's back?" No again. "Where have these people who voted been living or visiting?" Ellsworth wondered rhetorically. He did find some solace in an eight-page photo essay in the magazine's December 1998 issue by Big Empty photographer Wyman Meinzer of Benjamin that shows "how really attractive this area of West Texas really is." The essay was called "Flat Is Where It's At."

Perhaps Guthrie schoolteacher Joy Cave was right on target when, with a trace of defiance, she once declared: "We don't belong to anybody. We belong to ourselves."

18

When the discovery of oil brought new folks and mounds of money, much of West Texas was a wide, sparsely populated expanse of cattle lands. It was ripe for cattle rustlers familiar with the long, strung-out herds that moved over the winding trails to market.

Of course, Hollywood immediately loved West Texas, portraying it as wild, warped, and woolly, an untamed land of cowboys, Indians, crooks, killers, con men, oil men, boozers, crazies, hookers, rowdies, and rattlesnakes. That's distorted, but not altogether wrong. In 1920, a Texas Ranger submitted his report on a cattle thief: "Mean as hell. Had to kill him." More recently, an Odessa resident was asked by his nephew why he owned sixteen guns. "Because I've got sixteen windows," replied the uncle.

J. W. "Hog Creek" Carruth, a Desdemona barber, always claimed there was oil beneath a creek running through his farm. By golly, he was right. Carruth later distributed literature far and wide showing a rainbow linking his barbershop to an oil field. He called it "The Amazing Story of 'Hog Creek' Carruth."

Then there was Amon G. Carter, who was made for West Texas. Or vice versa. Where else could a man preach cow chips as an energy source, buy a newspaper, strike oil, dress in a cowboy hat and six-shooters, give away millions, and prompt J. C. Penney to say: "Fort Worth is not where the West begins. The West begins where ever Amon Carter is."

Where else but West Texas would you find a go-for-broke, don't-give-a-damn entrepreneur like Clayton Williams, a displaced stripper like Candy Barr, a ranching legend like Watt Matthews, or an eccentric millionaire prankster like Stanley Marsh 3? Or an unpretentious superstar like quarterback Sammy Baugh, who became a rancher in Rotan, or a common-sense political heavyweight like Robert Strauss, a Stamford native? Or Red McCombs, reared in Spur, who made a fortune selling cars in San Antonio and then spent a chunk of it buying the NFL's Minnesota Vikings?

Where else would there be a frontier legend like Charles Goodnight, who fought Comanches with Sul Ross, invented the chuck wagon, and died in his nineties as an established authority on twentieth-century ranching economics? Or Hallie Stillwell, a rancher, teacher, and justice of the peace, who was the first woman on her husband's Big Bend ranch? She bore a twelve-pound son after forty-eight hours with no anesthesia, lived under the border threat of Pancho Villa, and once said, "I found out quickly that I was to live like a man, work like a man, and act like a man."

President Bush's son George pursued an oil fortune in Midland before becoming a

Hallie Crawford Stillwell, 1897-1997, Big Bend pioneer, rancher, teacher, and justice of the peace. "She became a legend in her own time," said Ross McSwain, columnist for the San Angelo Standard-Times.

baseball team owner in Dallas, our governor in Austin, and perhaps even our president in Washington.

Alan Bean was born in the Panhandle town of Wheeler in 1932. By 1969, he was standing on the moon with fellow Apollo 12 astronaut Charles Conrad in man's second lunar landing.

John T. Montford made his mark prosecuting thieves and rapists as Lubbock's D.A., then spent more than a decade in the Texas Senate. He left to become Texas Tech's first-ever chancellor, but he may someday be known as the state's foremost collector of spurs. If so, credit his uncle in Muleshoe, who gave Montford his first boyhood set.

And how about a whole town of millionaires? Not exactly, but forty-three residents of a small farming community shared a forty-seven-million-dollar lottery jackpot in 1996 and are known now as the Roby Millionaires. After paying the IRS piper, they settled debts, bought new pickups, and kept on farming. A high school coach missed the bonanza because he drove over to Rotan to visit his barber. A wonderful guy, he laughed when he retold the story and explained how he would forever be known as that "poor S.O.B. who got hisself a million-dollar haircut."

And then there's the group called the Republic of Texas, whose members insist Texas is still an independent nation. They got everyone's attention during a week-long armed standoff in 1997 with three hundred state troopers and Texas Rangers at their "embassy" in the rugged Davis Mountains in far West Texas. Afterward, when the group's leader, Richard McLaren, and a top lieutenant were convicted of organized criminal activity, a prosecutor was moved to say, "I think basically we've cut the head off the snake."

West Texans are not fond of outsiders, and often with good cause. Odessa was invaded by howling journalists when, according to a Washington-based antihandgun group, it surpassed New York City and Miami as the nation's most dangerous city. "For Murder Capital U.S.A., it isn't much," snipped *Newsweek. The New York Times* also weighed in, but the unkindest cut came from *Dallas Times Herald* columnist Molly Ivins. "For you neo-natives," she wrote, "Odessa is an armpit about thirty miles down the road from an equal armpit named Midland."

Community leaders were nonplussed. In West Texas fashion, Tom Nickell, the editor of the *Odessa American*, reflected: "Actually, we think we've been upgraded. Some people refer to another part of the anatomy."

Lubbock wasn't spared when TV host Johnny Carson visited in 1970. "The worst is over," an uppity *LIFE Magazine* writer said of Johnny's airport arrival. "He had inched along the narrow length of red carpet on the field, along the ranks of people lined up, gauntlet style, in the shimmering Texas heat, having his hand pumped constantly and his back slapped once or twice soundly." Then there was the perceived indignity of meeting the mayor, "plump and folksy, in steel-rimmed glasses and a shiny gold-brown suit." Hey, said Mayor W. D. "Dub" Rogers later, "I consider that a compliment."

The onslaught continued in 1981 when *The Washington Post, The Philadelphia Inquirer, Newsweek, The Wall Street Journal,* and *Time* followed the trail of John Hinckley, President Reagan's would-be assassin, to Texas Tech. "Academically modest," commented *Newsweek* of the school Hinckley sporadically attended. "Prosaic state-run university on the dusty flatlands of the Texas Panhandle," chirped the *Journal,* somehow managing to move Tech out of Lubbock to somewhere closer to Amarillo. It was the *Post*

Will Rogers and Soapsuds on the Texas Tech campus. Soapsuds's posterior is pointed toward rival Texas A&M.

that made the largest leap in context: "A penchant for guns hardly strikes anyone as ominous in free-wheeling Lubbock, where some university students carry guns to class . . ."

Guns to class?

One month to the day after Hinckley wounded the president, the following corrective appeared: "An article in the April 5 editions of *The Washington Post* presented an inaccurate depiction of Texas Tech University and the city in which the university is located, Lubbock. Texas Tech students do not carry guns to class, as the article stated, and the city itself is a quiet town with orderly and law-abiding citizens. There is no 'pistol-packing' tradition in Lubbock, as the article incorrectly implied."

After that, you'd think Texas Tech would be left alone. Think again. In 1985, *Sports Illustrated* called Tech's campus the ugliest in the whole United States. Writer Douglas Looney also anointed Austin, home of the Texas Longhorns, the "best town." The fury of Tech alumni would have died of natural causes if Looney had not struck again in 1987:

"Three years ago, we said in this space that Texas Tech has the ugliest campus. An avalanche of mail disputed this assertion. So we have looked at the school again, rechecked the photos and consulted experts. We are not too proud to admit our mistakes. This, however, was not one of them."

Pretty smug, huh? A former Tech student named Joel Brandenberger thought so and was not pleased. He discovered a sports story entitled "A Real Lulu in Lubbock" that was written eleven years before Looney's denunciation. The article hitting the newstands in November 1976, described the campus as "elegant." And the magazine in which it appeared? None other than Looney's *Sports Illustrated*.

For West Texans, life can be cruel. Once listing the state's worst occupations, *Texas Monthly* put "Life-long resident of Wichita Falls" in the top ten. That essentially equated living in Wichita Falls with being a salvage worker on the bomb range at Fort Hood and sexing newborn chicks at the poultry farms in Gonzales. Friendly fire erupted again in 1998 when Wichita Falls displaced Austin as the preseason home of the Dallas Cowboys. *Texas Monthly* writer Skip Hollandsworth, who grew up in Wichita Falls, railed about overweight topless dancers and the effects of the heat. "Your vision blurs and your legs start quivering like dying fish on hooks," he whined.

"Of course, it's hot here," retorted Carroll Wilson, the editor of Wichita Falls's daily, the *Times Record News*. "And that's the way we like it, us and 103,000 other souls who believe there's more to a city than interminable traffic tie-ups, indefatigable drug dealers and insufferably smug magazine editors." When the *Austin American-Statesman* ran an unflattering photo of a junkyard in the foreground of Wichita Falls' downtown, Wilson had his fill. He dispatched a reporter and photographer to Austin to unmask some Capital City eyesores and prove it was just as hot there in August as his hometown.

When they aren't feuding with outsiders, West Texans occasionally find cause to take a whack at their neighbors. Cattle barons fought sheepherders and then sodbusters. The quarrel between cowmen who used the open range and those who fenced it in was so rancorous the governor called a special legislative session in 1884. After Dimmit beat out Castro City to become the county seat of Castro County, lingering resentment prompted a gunfight between a man named Andrew McClelland and Ira Aten, a retired Texas Ranger.

They say the mule's behind on Muleshoe's monument is pointed toward Lubbock—on purpose. The statue of Will Rogers on Soapsuds adorning the entrance to the Texas Tech campus, Soapsuds stands at an odd angle. That's because *its* rear end is aimed toward Texas A&M University, 420 miles to the southeast.

A judge in El Paso claimed the salt flats below the Guadalupe Mountains for his own private preserve. When he tried to charge a fee for the salt, angry citizens ran him out of town. But the Salt War of 1877 did not end there. Mexicans who brought cart trains across the border for decades were also irate, so their nemesis, a contingent of Texas Rangers, was assigned to guard the flats. "Before the dispute reached a confused, tragic end," says the *Texas State Travel Guide*, "it had involved both Mexican and U.S. citizens, political parties, judges, legislators, mob action, army troops, and Texas Rangers. Murder, assassinations and revenge killings took place on both sides."

More recently, the Pecos Independent School District annexed the schools in nearby Toyah in a secret meeting. To Toyah's 294 residents, the 1970 action was nothing less than an enemy invasion. No shots were fired, but a sign on Interstate 20 said "Welcome to Toyah—the Little Czechoslovakia of Reeves Co.," alluding to Russian aggression in eastern Europe about the same time.

Midland maintained that Odessa stole its state university, so it slashed the "Odessa" from what was originally the Midland-Odessa Regional Airport Terminal. Odessa, it was once alleged, dumped its sewage in Midland County. Odessa residents cringe when they hear Midland owns the oil wells and Odessa works on them. "You raise a family over there," observed an Odessa divorcee with two kids. "You raise hell over here." Then, the oil bust of the early 1980s inspired a call for a

cease-fire. The cities' media pledged a million dollars for a campaign whose theme was, "Midland and Odessa. We're Better Together."

Détente in the desert? Well, they unveiled a "friendship monument" at the University of Texas of the Permian Basin to stand as an enduring reminder of the cities' newfound camaraderie. A new freeway linked the northern sections of the old antagonists. Even so, a *Midland Reporter-Telegram* subscriber wrote, "Please pardon my lack of enthusiasm for the Permian Basin Media Coalition."

Dave Lyons, publisher of the *Odessa American,* said, "Hell, they're trying to get Odessa and Midland to get along and I can't even get east Odessa and west Odessa together." When the remark appeared in print, Lyons's readers howled about the reference to their own town, not Midland. He backtracked, claiming he was "misquoted out of context" by another one of those trouble-making out-of-town reporters.

And what about the love-in between Odessa and Midland? Attorney Mike McLeaish suggested with a grin, "Leave the university here in Odessa but change the name to the University of Texas at Midland." At last report, that hadn't happened. Neither had Odessa been restored to the name of the Midland Airport.

Nothing raises West Texans' ire more often than Washington bureaucrats. Said a rancher about a 1972 federal ban on poison: "We can put a man on the moon, but we can't kill a coyote." Another West Texan grumped: "It's a classic case of the coyote being put on welfare."

The federal government's most vociferous critics are in the oil business. "Every day, some S.O.B. is sitting up there in Washington trying to figure a new way to tax them, new

Salt Flats east of El Paso. Many thought they were worth fighting for.

ways to shaft them," a Midland executive once said.

Plainview was nailed by the Environmental Protection Agency for water quality. The federal agency was offended by the condition of a mostly dry gully near town over which it declared jurisdiction. Why? Because the gully was "a navigable water of the United States," no different from the mighty Mississippi.

Then there's the endangered golden-cheeked warbler, whose habitat is salt cedar. The infernal bushes gulp water by the barrel, but whacking them down is a big no-no where the warbler is concerned.

Thanks to the feds, a tiny snake delayed construction of a West Texas reservoir. The Concho water snake, it turned out, was thriving instead of threatened. The construction of Lake Ivie depended on a ten-year snake census because the federal government believed

only a relative handful existed. The snake census was conducted by teams of experts poking through weeds and turning over thousands of rocks. When the snakes were caught, they had to be measured, weighed, and massaged to determine their sex. They were injected with minute transponders so that— God forbid—no snake would be counted twice.

"Instead of just eight hundred snakes," wrote the *Abilene Reporter-News,* "there may be as many as seventy thousand of the critters cavorting in West Central Texas, swimming, eating tiny fish, and most significantly, making baby snakes." Among the now discarded federal recommendations: the construction of expensive alternative habitats along the Concho, which critics called snake condos. Okla Thornton, a biologist, said he pestered the U.S. Fish and Wildlife Service

Jack Ryan's saloon in the frontier town of Tascosa. Tascosa flourished on the west side of the Panhandle and Mobeetie prospered on the east side in the late 1800s, both adding to the Wild West reputation of the region.

for six years about the serpentine folly, but "it was almost as if it went in one ear and out the other."

Then, there was the county commissioner in the Panhandle community of Hereford who complained: "I got my taxes fighting my taxes." A 1980 newspaper headline succinctly summarized the issue: "Harvard vs. Hereford." That was because federally funded Texas Rural Legal Aid had set out its shingle in the farming and feedlot community. Ivy League law school graduates manned the barricades. On behalf of Hispanic laborers, the TRLA sued almost everybody in sight—the sheriff, the hospital, the Immigration and Nationalization Service, the housing authority, local politicians—and overturned a local school board election. "I'd like to be loved by everyone," said a baby-faced, bearded TRLA lawyer. "I'd also like to see justice done."

The strangest federal case had nothing to do with snakes, coyotes, or salt cedars. It occurred in 1989 in the unassuming town of Snyder when innkeeper Jack Pointeau did it right, which was wrong. You see, Jack entered the United States legally from his native France by obtaining a visa. He settled in Snyder and invested in the local Travelodge. His children graduated with honors from high school, his wife graduated magna cum laude from college, and he even joined Rotary. His investment, stung by the latest oil bust, did not turn out as well, but he kept the motel afloat with hard work and innovation.

When it came time to renew his visa, the federal immigration office in Dallas said no. Arbitrarily, his new friends in Snyder thought. Ironically, if he and his family had been living illegally in the United States for such an extended period, he already would have been granted amnesty under the latest immigration reform laws. Eventually the authorities relented and Jack and his family stayed. The editor of the *Snyder Daily News*, Donny Brown, summed it up best: "This is a Catch-22 bureaucratic boondoggle."

An out-of-stater said, "You Texans look down on other people, don't you?" The rancher drawled, "Not that I know of—but we sure as hell don't look up to anybody."

Boyce House, *Texas Proud*, 1943

4

Whether cursing them or kissing them, West Texans are not above taking outsiders' help. New York money fed many an oil strike. None other than Charles Goodnight, the Texas Panhandle's ranching deity, had a boss, an Englishman named John George Adair. Adair "was an overbearing son-of-a-gun," snorted Goodnight, "and would have been beaten up several times if it hadn't been for me." The good fortune was Goodnight's. Originally without a spread to call his own, he acquired 140,000 acres and twenty thousand cattle in a settlement with Adair's estate. And lived "intensely and amply" until the age of ninety-three, noted biographer J. Evetts Haley.

It's painful to admit, but the Texas Capitol in Austin could not be built without foreigners' cash in exchange for a colossal chunk of West Texas—more than three million acres, give or take a county or two. Two Chicago boys, Charles and John Farwell, fronted for the Capitol Freehold Land & Investment Company, incorporated in Great Britain. They created the famed XIT, whose northern and southern fences were separated by two hundred miles. Piddling when compared to the XIT, the Matador Land and Cattle Co. was established by a Scottish syndicate in 1882. A mere million acres, it was.

Every Texas Ranger had to wear a Stetson, designed in 1870 by John Batterson Stetson of Philadelphia. His factory was producing four million cowboy hats a year when he died in 1906.

C. W. Post made his money in cereal, then arrived in West Texas to create an economic utopia, the town of Post. It survives today with fewer than four thousand souls.

Amarillo announced a startling offer to 1,350 U.S. companies in 1995: Bring us eight hundred jobs and we will pay you eight million dollars. Someone should have whispered, "Be careful what you wish for." An office furniture supplier agreed to shut its doors in Coleman in exchange for a $1.5 million relocation grant and other favors. Then the *Amarillo Globe-News* discovered the owner used sixty-five thousand dollars to purchase a home—in the verdant, forested East Texas city of Longview. In 1998, Amarillo's aggressiveness paid off. It snatched Bell Helicopter's new tilt-rotor plant from several larger rivals.

No one knows for certain how Orrin Shaid Jr. found Melvin, population 205, in sheep

Charles Goodnight, pioneer Panhandle rancher. Cowboys and Native Americans were invited by Goodnight to participate in a staged buffalo hunt in 1916 on the ranch where Goodnight preserved a buffalo herd.

and goat country near Brady. But they wish he hadn't. For a time, moribund Melvin sported a brand new bank, the Ranchlander, and a restaurant by the same name in a new native stone building. So what if the "owner," a tall blonde in a sleek limousine, would infrequently appear with a big, wavy-haired guy at the wheel. After bank examiners padlocked the Ranchlander, Melvin's citizens would come to know the chauffeur as Shaid, the real owner, and the blonde as his girlfriend, who lived in luxury at a lake home near Tyler. Shaid was convicted of nineteen counts of mail fraud, bank fraud, false statements, and bank robbery.

Borger was called the toughest city in the nation in 1930 by a historian, who noted, "There were people of every description and from every state . . . seeking riches or adventure." Named for local banker Ace Borger, the town virtually grew overnight to thirty thousand people in a 1920s oil boom. Borger was placed twice under martial law, requiring the attendance of Texas Rangers. Otherwise, it was ruled by "Two-Gun" Dick Heirig. "At that time, there was eight hundred and twenty-four joints running wide open under Dick's jurisdiction," wrote roustabout-author Slim Jones. "Eleven hundred and twenty-one slot machines; one thousand, two hundred and eighty wild women . . . Dick was to collect eighteen dollars a week from each of these women. The money that was collected other ways by his hijackers or robbers was fifty-fifty." Borger survives as a stable oil refining and chemical center, but the question remains: who counted all those wild women and slot machines?

Despite leader Richard McLaren's pleas, there was no massive influx of outsiders to Fort Davis in support of the Republic of Texas secessionists. The exception was seven fellows who aroused the suspicions of a truckstop waitress in Pecos. Shucks, they were just good ol' boys from East Texas on a hunting trip. Guess that explained the trunkload of semiautomatic rifles and ammunition.

Even when the crimes were not committed in West Texas, the trials somehow ended up there. The renowned sons of Dallas eccentric billionaire H. L. Hunt, Bunker and Herbert, were acquitted by a Lubbock jury of federal wiretapping charges. The Dallas millionaires were charged with eavesdropping on their father's employees.

Henry Lee Lucas, the one-eyed drifter who once claimed to have killed 360 people, received his only death sentence from a San Angelo jury. It was the famous Orange Socks case, called this because, sadly, that was the only clothing on a still unidentified woman whose body was found in a culvert in central Texas. "I feel like I've been to a Mad Hatter's tea party," said Lucas's lawyer. Among other curious developments, his client confessed to the crime, then said he lied about his startling confession. The San Angelo jury believed Lucas's first version.

The Sharpstown political scandal of the early 1970s was mostly an Austin affair, but the trial moved to Abilene when it came time to prosecute House Speaker Gus Mutscher and two of his cronies. It was a raucous courtroom saga with a former Miss America, Donna Axum of Arkansas, among the daily spectators. The shadow of Governor Preston Smith hung over the proceedings. A couple of flashy young lawyers were making names for themselves, although Richard "Racehorse" Haynes of Houston and Joe Shannon Jr. of Fort Worth were on the losing end. The jury found Mutscher and his co-defendants guilty of conspiracy to commit bribery.

Governor Smith was never charged in the scandals, although he was branded in the Abilene courtroom one madcap morning as an unindicted co-conspirator. A reporter, defying the judge's explicit instructions, jumped up and raced for the phones. In his haste, he stuck his arm through the glass portion of the courtroom door, shattering it. For a few fitful moments, the press corps feared it would be permanently banished from the proceedings. Fortunately, the judge was so angry he was struck speechless. Mutscher and the other convicted defendants never spent a day in jail. In fact, good ol' Gus eventually returned home to East Texas, ran for county judge and got himself elected!

While eventful, the Sharpstown trial in Abilene was a sideshow compared to the marathon trial of Cullen Davis, at the time the richest man in U.S. history to be tried for murder. Davis was accused of being the "man in black" who gunned down four people, killing two, in a post-midnight massacre at his six-million-dollar mansion in Fort Worth in August 1976. The first to die was the twelve-year-old daughter of Cullen's estranged wife, Priscilla. Also killed was Stan Farr, Priscilla's thirty-year-old live-in boyfriend. Priscilla herself was critically wounded, as was a young mansion visitor, Bubba Gavrel. After a mistrial in Fort Worth, the case was moved to a supposedly neutral site in Amarillo amid great fanfare. Groupies descended on the Potter County Courthouse en masse each day, bringing cakes, cookies, and other goodies to Cullen and his defense team, headed by Racehorse Haynes.

Racehorse treated spectators to an incredible performance, attacking Priscilla's credibility and lifestyle. It was a thinly camouflaged attempt to divert the jury's attention away from his client and the devastating evidence presented by the prosecution. Haynes paraded a slew of "scuzzies and scalawags" to the witness stand and did his dead-level best to portray them as Priscilla's friends, associates, or lovers. The citizens of Amarillo, while hardly pristine, had never seen anything like it.

One of the leading characters in this notorius Panhandle trial was the judge, George Dowlen. Judge George spent most days trying to keep Haynes from showing lewd photographs of Priscilla's motorcycle-racing boyfriend to bewildered jurors. And he spent most nights entertaining visiting reporters and a covey of comely lasses at a popular nightspot called Rhett Butler's.

Ultimately, the jury spurned the testimony of three eyewitnesses to the mansion carnage and acquitted Cullen of capital murder. Afterward, a couple of panel members and a bailiff or two joined Cullen at Rhett's for a victory celebration. So did Judge George, which raised a few eyebrows. The party was such a success that Cullen tossed a luncheon for the entire jury the next day at the Hilton Hotel where the prosecution team was headquartered.

Racehorse, meanwhile, set the tone for the post-trial high jinks. Flushed with success and a sizeable amount of Scotch, and peering into the cameras and microphones of the West Texas media, he dismissed Priscilla as a "shameless, brazen hussy . . . a charlatan, a harlot and a liar . . . a snake, unworthy of belief under oath . . . a habitué of dope." Haynes listened in painful disbelief the next morning as a colleague recounted the events of the previous evening. "Did I really call her a harlot?" he moaned.

Once a justice, always a justice.

Judge Roy Bean

5

The reckless spirit and extreme solitude of West Texas frequently are reflected in West Texans such as Judge Roy Bean of Langtry, the "Law West of the Pecos." The judge, with his beer-drinking bear at his side, once fined a dead man all the money he had on him. Got him for loitering.

As the years passed, the laughter faded somewhat for Stanley Marsh, best known for burying a fleet of ten Cadillacs nose down, fins up along old Route 66 outside Amarillo. More recently, his mock street signs (Steal This Sign; Big Deal; Blood) rekindled his on-again, off-again feud with Amarillo's equally rich and prominent Whittenburg family. "He uses his signs as an attractive nuisance to lure—and then compromise and threaten —teenaged boys into doing his bidding," alleged a lawsuit filed by the Whittenburgs. A special prosecutor also brought five felony counts, including kidnapping. Marsh denied the charges, which dated back to 1994.

It was the spring of 1998 when Marsh appeared briefly before visiting District Judge Don Lane in the courthouse in Amarillo. At age sixty, an adult life of eccentricity already behind him, he pleaded no contest to reduced charges of unlawful restraint and trespassing, both misdemeanors. The details of the formal charge were curious, to say the least. Marsh, who built a small broadcasting empire, stood accused of locking teenager Benjamin Burkhart Whittenburg in a chicken coop. Stanley's plea bargain cost him four thousand dollars and ten days in jail, although the judge agreed to a defense request for community service.

"I prefer 'individualistic' to 'eccentric,'" Stanley Marsh 3 once said. The "3" behind his surname is, as you would expect, correct. When it came to the world-famous Cadillacs, Marsh was a tad modest. He credited a group of California artists calling themselves the Ant Farm with the concept and the construction of the partially buried cars. "I own the Cadillac Ranch only in the sense that it is on my family's land," his prepared statement read. "The Cadillac Ranch is an art piece and the rights to its use belong only to its creators." For some reason, the Cadillacs were stuck in their concrete sheaths at the exact angles of the Great Pyramid. Each represents a tail-fin model dating from the original in 1956 to the phased-out versions in the mid-60s. "The Cadillac symbolizes your fantasy," Stanley said. "It was the total dream . . . The Cadillac Ranch is the celebration of that dream."

Another Marsh dream was to float a mountain, but it only partially worked. The

Stanley Marsh 3 and the famous buried Cadillacs on his ranch west of Amarillo

idea was to wrap a section of a hill near his hometown in metal, designed to blend into the pale Panhandle sky. The top would seem disconnected from the base of the hill, giving the illusion of a floating mountain top. But the most common reaction was, "Huh?"

Then, there was the work of art that could be fully appreciated only from an airplane: a gigantic pool table fashioned from a grassy field with forty-two-inch stuffed "balls" surrounded by a fence to keep the cows out.

Some concluded that his masterpiece was three letters of the alphabet propped against a fence. They spelled A-R-T.

Stanley's pranks, while not always appreciated, were mostly amusing. He once stashed a skunk in the dressing quarters of the bride and bridesmaids at an elegant wedding. He also stuffed his favorite pig, Minnesota Fats, after it overdosed on chocolate. And he tossed a reception for Japanese

businessmen at his home, Toad Hall, and invited no Texan shorter than six-foot-four. When a correspondent for the Weather Channel went live with a report on Amarillo's late-season blizzard in 1999, Stanley donned a buffalo headdress and did an unscheduled snow dance in the background.

He rated his own chapter in a book entitled *Texas Big Rich,* which described a satirical letter he wrote to Pat Nixon. So the story goes, he had heard she was upset that her husband forbade her to wear fur hats while he was president. Stanley's letter evidently landed him on Richard Nixon's enemies' list. *Texas Big Rich* says he was audited and the licenses for his television stations were delayed. Whatever, Nixon eventually apologized.

If some people are born showmen or born politicians, then Billie Sol Estes was a born promoter. A born West Texas promoter. "You can shear a lamb every year," he was fond of saying, "but you can only skin it once." Estes was no doubt the best-known fertilizer salesman in Texas. Once a Pecos entrepreneur and Democratic confidant of Lyndon Johnson, Estes settled in Brady in his twilight years. At the time of this writing, he still was wheeling and dealing despite two federal prison stints and several other brushes with the law.

In her book, *Billie Sol: King of the Texas Wheeler Dealers,* daughter Pam Estes recalled the champagne days in Pecos, before his fraudulent fertilizer tanks and the nasty allegations—the days when Lyndon Johnson and Ralph Yarborough and other political bigwigs were Billie Sol's buddies and beneficiaries of Estes's largess; before the 1960s convictions for mail fraud and conspiracy to defraud; before the 1979 convictions for fraud and concealing assets; before the eleven years behind bars in a variety of federal prisons; before the slow crumble and eventual collapse of a desert empire of land, cotton, cattle, oil, and businesses, including even a daily newspaper.

"Like rich people everywhere, we live in a big house run by efficient servants," Pam wrote. "I am in my lilac bedroom designed for a princess, and even though I'm not old enough to have a driver's license, my own purple Cadillac is downstairs in its parking place waiting for me. Washington politicians have just flown in for one of Daddy's 'two-oxen barbecues' . . . It seems for awhile that Pecos is the crossroads for Democratic Party financial strategy."

Abandoned adobe store, Langtry, 1982

In 1983, just as Billie Sol was being released for the second time from a federal prison, a reporter visited Pecos to see what folks had to say about their most famous citizen. "Some people think he did a lot for Pecos, and a lot of others think he was a crook," said a resident named Randy McWhirter, who actually was right on both counts. Declared Mary Bessent: "He was not a native. He was just a big shot who came here to put together a deal. He left a lot of the farmers broke . . . damaged the economy . . . and ruined the reputation of the town."

Daughter Pam, pushing fifty and a delightfully crafty chip off the old block, would recall her father once told her: "The thing I am guilty of is being insane. I had it made when I was twenty-five, but I was always greedy and wanted more, and I ended up losing it all." Later, in prison, Billie Sol explained that he was haunted by a history of bizarre and ill-fated compulsions, a form of insanity he said persisted even to that day. "I'm one of the unfortunates," he claimed. "I'm just one drink away from being a drunk and just one deal away from being back in prison. I'm a compulsive person. I'm a compulsive drinker, and if I smoked, I'd be a compulsive smoker. Anything I've done, it's been compulsive."

Estes once estimated his fortune at between $150 million and $400 million, which is quite a disparity, but then he always did think big. In a prison interview in Big Spring in the early '80s, Billie Sol bemoaned the fact that he never turned the Pecos Valley into the wine capital of the world. "My plan was to put the land in grapes and pecans. You'll see the day when that whole valley will be in grapes. We were just twenty years ahead of our time." If he were a young man, he said, he would still do it. "It would be real feasible and real profitable and the financing would be real easy to obtain . . . We could, truly, move the wine business from France to West Texas, and I've got some people who would like for me to go out there and do that." A

moment later, with a sigh and shrug, he added: "I know I could make it work, but I don't want to work that hard and that long."

When he got out of jail that time, or, for that matter, any time, he insisted he was a changed man. "I'm ready to go, ready to get out," he said. "I'm just going to live a day at a time and not worry about tomorrow. My values have completely changed. You may not believe me but when I left prison I left a part of me behind. I leave with no bitterness or malice toward anyone. This is just a bend in the road of my life. Not the end of my life . . . When I was out of prison before, I was an empire builder. Money, money, money. I've seen myself as a Robin Hood back then. I'd take from the rich and give to the poor. I heard the cry of the poor and I answered the cry of the poor . . . God being my helper, I'm just going home and help Pam sell her book."

Whatever his plans, he subsequently stirred up a hornet's nest when he told a grand jury that the late President Johnson ordered the 1961 slaying of a U.S. Department of Agriculture official. Confirming reports leaked to three Texas newspapers, Robertson County District Attorney John Paschall said Estes told grand jurors that Johnson ordered the killing of Henry Marshall because the USDA official could have linked the then-vice president to Estes's illegal activities. However, Paschall pointed out that the unsubstantiated testimony by Estes was not endorsed by the grand jury.

Marshall was an upper level official in a federal agency that oversaw cotton-growing licenses in Texas. He was shot to death in June 1961 on his farm in Franklin, 120 miles south of Dallas. Several of Johnson's former associates disputed the Estes allegations and one denounced him as a publicity seeking "pathological liar." The uproar coincided with the release of Pam's book, which dealt largely with her childhood remembrances of her father and shed little light on Billie Sol's darker side.

Billie Sol Estes, con man and presidential confidant

That darker side surfaced again a year later when he was accused of assault by a thirty-eight-year-old widow who had come to Abilene to be Billie Sol's housekeeper. The charge subsequently was dismissed, and Estes maintained long thereafter that the woman's allegations were unfounded and that prosecutors would have "looked like complete fools" if they had taken the case to trial.

By the late '90s, with no new jail stints but a couple of near misses, Billie Sol and Patsy, the ultimate long-suffering wife, were living in Brady on the northern fringe of the Hill Country. The Texas attorney general's office had filed but later dropped criminal charges against Estes in connection with what Billie Sol insisted were charitable operations in Abilene.

Billie Sol sat down with a reporter in late 1997 to discuss the "good old days," a book he's been threatening to write for years, and a movie that's been in the works forever, and maybe longer. A bit plumper, his bushy graying mane and familiar horned-rim glasses intact, he still fractured the King's English as his mouth raced to keep up with his mind. "I don't usually talk to reporters," he volunteered. "The young ones don't even know World War II ended. They don't know Texas history. They don't know Texas politics. They don't know nothin'. They don't have no Texas roots."

At the time, Washington was in a dither over its latest money-raising scandal, and Billie Sol was grumbling that the current capital gang couldn't hold a crooked candle to the politicians of his era. "Back then, people had power and used that power. They could make a decision and they could get it done. They lived by their own set of rules." He indicated those ancient rules included suitcases stuffed with cash. His voice dropping to a conspiratorial whisper, he revealed his involvement in a movie project that he said he just couldn't discuss. "It's going to bring out a lot of the truth," he insisted. "There had to be a lot of deaths before it could be done. What they're interested in is not Billie Sol. It's the history of the era. Billie Sol is just a little bitty wheeler-dealer in Texas."

Still, he pointed out, he was "at the party" and knows what went on. "I could have wrapped some things around their necks," he asserted without disclosing what things or whose necks. "I'd been dead if I did it, or even hinted at it." Actually, he confessed, flashing his best wily old fox grin, "I'm just lucky to be alive, knowing what I know."

Then there was the late Tom "Pinkie" Roden. As crafty and cunning as a coyote, Pinkie was a shy, gentle, stuttering, freckle-faced, enigmatic hulk who grew up dirt poor, made a fortune on illegal whiskey and then founded the most curious and far flung, legal liquor store chain in all of Texas. Whether beloved as a civic godfather or implicated in a farm family's tragedy, he cast a long shadow over his West Texas homeland. During his earlier days, investigators quietly bought his souped-up used cars so they might occasionally have a chance of catching one of his drivers. Later, in his prime, Pinkie could be found socializing with governors or shooting dice with legendary gamblers such as Duck Mallard. "He drove us crazy," said the late Coke Stevenson Jr., once the state liquor board administrator and an improbable admirer. "But I couldn't help but like him."

Friends called him Pinkie, "The Wizard of the West," and they called him often. They called him when they needed money, jobs, donations, legal advice, political clout, or maybe just a good bottle of whiskey or a large or small dice game. They called him from the state capital in Austin or from a sleazy jail in West Texas. "Anytime you needed something done, you could count on Pinkie getting it done," said an oilman named Charles Perry. Politicians privately sought his counsel and his contributions, and it was former Governor Preston Smith of Lubbock who said: "I would class Tom Roden as one of the top ten people I know."

The Odessa Chamber of Commerce installed him in its Business Hall of Fame and a former state whiskey regulator praised him as "an outstanding citizen, a great character, a dear friend, and the kingpin of the liquor business in Texas for many years." His adopted hometown of Odessa, the rowdy West Texas oil mecca, honored him as its outstanding citizen. Not bad for a guy who did hard time at the state prison in his younger days and amassed a fortune bootlegging whisky to thirsty West Texans before turning legit.

Still, few really knew him, for he was passionately private. Much of his life was a mystery, which was what he wanted. And yet, insiders suggest Pinkie Roden was bigger than life, a civic and political godfather flawed by a dark side and a shadowy past. Both a legal and illegal beer and whiskey merchant, he was an outlaw, even his widow once conceded; but "a good outlaw, an outlaw with heart." At his death in 1989, Pinkie's longtime friend John Ben Sheppard, a former state attorney general, declared: "We'll never know the extent of his contributions or philanthropy. He let others take the bows, and he did the work and paid the bills."

Even so, a little girl from the South Plains grew up loathing him, convinced that he murdered her parents, though indirectly. When, in womanhood, she learned the whole story, it didn't much change her opinion.

Pinkie bought and renovated a dying hotel in downtown Odessa, christened it the Inn of the Golden West, decorated it with a glitzy penthouse nightclub and immortalized it with illegal casino-style gambling. "Before liquor by the drink, the Golden Rooster was the premier club in this state," said Gene

Tom "Pinkie" Roden, West Texas's civic godfather, cast a long and sometimes dark shadow.

Garrison, a longtime friend of Pinkie's. "This was especially true when the seventh floor was operative. There was no reason to go to Las Vegas. It was all right here."

Pinkie first settled in Big Spring, which permitted the legal sale of liquor and allowed him a perfect source and front for his bootlegging activities. But the good folks in Big Spring struck a surprise blow for temperance in the '50s, voting the city "dry" while other cities were going "wet." Pinkie was not pleased, though he learned a valuable lesson. Never again would he be blindsided by a political election, an episode that left him feeling more than a little vindictive. "If it stays dry, I'll still be selling whiskey in Big Spring, you know that," Pinkie reportedly told Police Chief Pete Green.

But Pinkie moved his budding liquor empire literally lock, stock, and barrel sixty miles west to Odessa and never looked back. He would eventually reopen a Big Spring store when the town reversed its dry vote, but he had found a home in Odessa. Instinctively, Pinkie knew it was his kind of town, young and brash and prone to wink at any law that might intrude on the good times.

Perhaps the last of his special if not always noble breed, his legacy will be with Texas for generations to come. Like no other, he used his political influence to shape the crazy-quilt laws governing how, where, what, and when Texans buy and drink their alcohol. That was after he spent a couple of decades outwitting the Texas Rangers and other law enforcement agencies, as much for fun as profit.

"He was the best," the late Coke Stevenson Jr. told a reporter one day in Austin. "Pinkie had the smartest drivers and the fastest cars and his people were loyal to a fault."

Stevenson, once a liquor board administrator, recalled a meeting in which an officer appealed for new, bigger and faster cars to challenge Pinkie's backroad bootlegging activities. Told that such funding was not available, Stevenson said the agent then asked for money to buy Pinkie's used cars and equipment. "They're better than anything we've got," he insisted. Stevenson maintained that Pinkie could drive better in the dark than in daylight, and that he could travel from Odessa to Dallas without using a major highway. "He knew the back roads of West Texas better than most people know the backyards of their home," he laughed.

When a woman named Elva Jo Edwards read that line in a 1991 news story, she was infuriated, and rightfully so. Forty years earlier, she was an infant passenger in a car that collided with a souped-up sedan loaded with bootleg beer and whiskey. The sedan was traveling at night without lights on a remote West Texas road between Brownfield and Tahoka, Elva's hometown. Elva was only a year old at the time and her sister was three. Their mother, father, and maternal grandmother were killed in the crash, as were two of three adults in the second car. The only survivor was a driver who worked for Pinkie Roden.

Elva grew up with only a vague idea of what occurred that spring night in 1951 but believing that Pinkie somehow was responsible for the killing of her parents. The article on Pinkie that appeared in 1991 triggered an odyssey that took Elva time and again from her home in Colorado back to Texas in search of the truth. And in 1999, when she finally met with the author who wrote the stories about Pinkie, she had one particularly penetrating question. "What I want to know," she asked, "is where are the stories about the pain Pinkie caused?"

6

"I love Texas, I really do."

Candy Barr, 1970, at a court hearing on marijuana charges in Brownwood, her former hometown

Brownwood seems the quintessential West Texas city, which is a bit odd, because its lineage is suspect and it's not overrun with oil rigs. It was founded on land donated by a farmer named Greenleaf Fisk, and its first mayor was named Q. C. Crump. It once was Apache territory, but the Comanches displaced the Apaches, who in turn were removed by the U.S. Army in 1874-75.

Brownwood is a showcase for West Texas illogic: You must be a "member" of a private club to buy a mixed drink, but anyone can purchase a truckload of booze at the town's liquor stores. A creek runs through town, which sounds idyllic. But it's usually dry until the first heavy rainfall. Then it floods, not unlike creeks in sister cities all across the region.

Brownwood is home to a splendidly daft undertaker named Groner Pitts and a motel that once claimed to be "The Best Little Snorehouse in Texas." But it is best known for Coach Gordon Wood's schoolboy football teams.

Wood started his championship string at Stamford, added seven state titles at Brownwood, and retired as the winningest high school coach in America. "There is nothing that will pull a whole town together like a good football team," said Wood, whose buddies in Brownwood and across West Texas would be quick to agree. "There's just something about a winning football team, especially in a little town," said Brownwood builder Herman Bennett. "When Gordon Wood got here and we started winning, everyone got behind the team and the town. Even the town started growing."

And then there's Brownwood's Candy Barr, gone now but not forgotten. Perhaps the Lone Star state's most notorious stripper, Candy was a headliner at Abe Weinstein's Colony Club and the toast of Big D's darker side in the freewheeling '50s. "I named her, started her in business, managed her," Weinstein bragged. "She packed the house every night." After a nasty little drug bust, Candy drifted out to Brownwood and eventually into self-imposed anonymity.

Not to pick on Brownwood, but its residents heartily proclaim their West Texas heritage while living next to the geographical center of the state.

"Groner's got a strange and weird perception of things," a friend of Brownwood's most famous mortician once said. The friend, Charlie Trigg, knew firsthand of Groner Pitt's escapades.

When singer Anita Bryant was embroiled in a gay rights controversy and her popularity suspect, Groner picked her to star in a July 4 celebration. Surprisingly, twenty thouand folks attended on short notice.

To his wife's dismay, he once used his living room to exhibit a prize bull.

Groner served as a campaign chairman for the late Texas Governor John Connally, appearing in Austin one day to cajole his candidate. "He took me to an embalmer's convention," Connally said. "He even showed me how they did it."

When Lieutenant Governor Ben Barnes lost a race for governor, Groner tried to cheer him up. Upon Barnes's return to Brownwood, he was greeted with fire trucks, a marching band, National Guard tanks, and a parade. The mayor spoke, Groner showered Barnes with gifts, and then he invited everyone to Barnes's home for hot dogs and refreshments. Later, the undertaker presented Barnes with a bill for the whole shebang, including the gifts. Disarmed by such audacity, Barnes paid it.

Both Connally and Barnes served as roasters at a Groner Pitts You're a Great American Day in Brownwood. And Barnes finally got a measure of revenge. Without checking, he invited the fifteen hundred

Carolyn LeMay displays hats she is making for sale, Brownwood.

Groner Pitts, Brownwood undertaker, at the Good Shepherd Memorial in his funeral home's cemetery

persons attending the roast to Groner's well-appointed home for post-roast cocktails. Most showed up.

Gordon Wood walked like a listing ship, and there was always paint or ink or some mysterious smudge decorating his best dress slacks. He talked funny, like maybe through his nose, and he could eat grass like a goat, especially when excited, which was most of the time. He resembled a kindly but disheveled teddy bear, and he lapped up coffee like a giant sponge.

And in West Texas, Gordon Wood was as identifiable with schoolboy football as Bear Bryant was with the colleges and Vince Lombardi with the pros. His triumphs included nine state championships, more than four hundred victories, and membership in every hall of fame and hall of honor except fashion and hair styling. In what ranks as an all-time upset, he once received a cultural award, causing a surprised assistant to drawl, "Shucks, Coach, you can't even spell culture."

It all began in the 1930s in the small West Texas town of Rule. Young Gordon Wood emerged from the cotton fields to take his first head coaching job. Actually, jobs. "I coached football, track, and basketball and didn't have a single assistant," he remembered. He won eleven games and lost nine before Uncle Sam's Navy interrupted his civilian activities. "I'd never even seen a ship, let alone been on one," he once told an interviewer.

Returning to West Texas in 1945, he hired on at Roscoe, where his teams were 17-2-2 and won a district championship. "I was also the high school principal and taught three math classes," he said with a warped grin. "I coached football, basketball, and track and drove a school bus in the morning. And I still didn't have an assistant." Of course, with that fat $185-a-month salary, one could hardly demand a bed of roses.

From there it was on to Seminole, where his football team was 20-9-2 and a one-man track team named Val Joe Walker won him his first state championship. "What events did Walker win?" a visitor wondered. "Any ones he wanted to," was the reply.

After a 7-3 season at Winters, Wood launched his first dynasty at Stamford, which was 81-6 in seven years including six district titles and two state championships. There, players such as Wayne Wash, Bob Harrison, Mike McClellan, Kenneth Lowe and Charlie Davis were all-state. Wash, son of cafe owner Nat Wash, went to University of Texas, Harrison and Mike McClellan to University of Oklahoma, Lowe to SMU, and Davis to McMurry College in Abilene. Harrison would become Wood's first all-American.

"I have great memories of Stamford," Wood said. "The things those kids went on to achieve is unbelievable, actually phenomenal." A writer for *The New York Times* once visited Wood at his Brownwood home while researching a story on academics versus athletics. With more than casual pride, Wood produced a photograph of one of his Stamford teams and began to list the players' accomplishments. "This one's a lawyer, this one's a doctor, this one's a coach, this one's a college professor, this one's a business executive . . ." Wood recalled with obvious delight. "I get your point," the writer conceded.

After leaving Stamford, Wood spent two years at Victoria (17-2-2) before settling in at Brownwood for the long haul. And his teams there were even more successful than those at Stamford, at least on the field. As head coach and athletic director, Wood's Lions were 257-52-7 and won nine state titles. When he retired in 1985 at age seventy-one, his 405 victories made him the nation's winningest coach. Some say his 405-88-12 record, which is a winning percentage of .814, may never be equaled.

"Actually, if I did what I wanted to do, I'd go after Alonzo Stagg's record. I think he coached seventy-two years, or something like that. I really would. I think that would be a challenge," he said. But after forty-three years, he concluded, the time had come to step down. And if he had it all to do over, he'd do the same thing. "I guarantee you I'd be a football coach," he said with that familiar crooked grin. "It's the finest thing in the world . . . I have no regrets."

Gordon Wood, football coach, with another legend behind him

Gordon Wood, coach of the Brownwood Lions, is carried off the field by his team after his 300ᵗʰ win.

Just think of it—riding 650 miles from nowhere to nowhere."

Thomas Jackson, *I'm from Texas, You Can't Steer Me,* 1907

7

Defining the essence of West Texas is no more difficult than pinpointing its eastern boundary, which is impossible. All agree, however, that Dallas and its sophisticated glitter are not included. Despite the geographical imbalance, Fort Worth, the City Where the West Begins, has no choice but to be in West Texas. That designation conveniently ignores the fact that the Louisiana border is only two hundred miles east of Fort Worth, whereas El Paso is a distant six hundred miles west.

The erstwhile West Texas Chamber of Commerce once drew its line from Gainesville south to Fort Worth and Waco to just west of Austin and San Antonio and on down to Del Rio on the Mexican border. "All of these towns are eastern extremities," said the chamber's executive vice president at the time, Adolph Janca. Using Janca's yardstick, West Texas includes 132 of the state's 254 counties and encompasses 159,601 square miles. That's three times the size of New York and larger than New Mexico, New Jersey, and New Hampshire combined, with Rhode Island and Delaware thrown in. More importantly, Janca's organization cleverly annexed Kerrville and much of the Texas Hill Country. That's not the same as Nevada grabbing up San Francisco, New Jersey laying claim to Boston, or Arkansas nabbing New Orleans. But it's close.

West Texans don't have to travel to Florida to find Miami or to Tennessee to visit Memphis, both of which are in the Panhandle. For that matter, there's no need to cross an ocean to locate Dublin. There's also an Eden and a Nazareth in West Texas, but the latter's known less for its Biblical ties than its basketball teams.

Levelland is in fact level and the view from Plainview is indeed plain. But did you know Plainview's most famous high school dropout is the founder of Netscape? Jim Clark's his name.

There's a literary trail, so to speak, of Tennyson, Bronte, Dryden, and even Dickens. There's a Wink, a Draw, a Star, a Loop, and a Wall. More fitting, perhaps, are Bronco, Lariat, Cactus, and Spur. Trees do grow in Notrees, and although there is no real lake in Big Lake, there still is a giant pool—of oil. The University of Texas owned much of the arid grazing land around Big Lake when the Santa Rita No. 1 blew in. The discovery made the university one of the richest schools in America, at the same time triggering an era of prosperity for much of West Texas. Vernon, headquarters of the Waggoner oil and ranching empire, was once known more colorfully as "Eagle Flats." Colorado City, which began as a Texas Ranger camp, later was called "The Tumbleweed Capital" of Texas.

Llano Estacado meant "staked plain" to early explorers. Now, it's the name of a West Texas vintner.

Surrounded by Abilene is the municipality of Impact, created for Abilene's tipplers before the city voted itself wet.

El Paso has its own nation—the Tiguas—who, in turn, have their own casino.

Marfa's got a multiple claim to fame, with its enchanting and mysterious mountain lights and a Texas thoroughbred named Marfa that raced in the 1983 Kentucky Derby. The horse lost, but not to worry. Movie buffs will long remember Marfa as the town that housed the cast of *Giant.*

Larry McMurtry, our semireclusive literary treasure, put Claude on the cinematic map with *Hud,* made from his book *Horseman, Pass By.* And he immortalized his hometown of Archer City with *The Last Picture Show.* He also won a Pulitzer Prize for Fiction for *Lonesome Dove,* in which he created two memorable characters in Texas Rangers Gus McRae and Woodrow Call.

After all the oil booms and busts, the biggest business in McMurtry's hometown of Archer City is books. Books of all kinds—new, old, used, and rare. Several buildings now house the collections, another example of McMurtry's enterprise. At the Chalk Hill

Downtown Tulia, Swisher County, 1999

Remuda on the Waggoner Ranch near Vernon, circa 1950

Grill, visiting bibliophiles sip gourmet soup alongside roughnecks with red mud on their boots who are devouring the chicken fried steak special. McMurtry's influence also spawned a bed-and-breakfast trade and weekends at the Spur Hotel for literary and musical retreats.

That's ironic, to say the least, because native son McMurtry was Public Enemy Number One when Hollywood came to Archer City to film *The Last Picture Show,* a tale about small-town kids coming of age in the '50s. Preachers denounced the book and the Oscar-nominated movie from the pulpit, and some old friends turned a chilly shoulder to members of McMurtry's clan. Curious residents drove three hours to Dallas to see the movie even though it was being shown just twenty-five miles up the road in Wichita Falls. They wanted to avoid being spotted by anyone who knew them. An Archer County probation officer named Gary Beesinger observed, "A lot of people didn't want it filmed here because of the moral issues raised in the book." That was probably an understatement, given the main characters' sexual appetites. "I still cringe at some of the scenes, but it moved me emotionally," admitted Beesinger, a Baptist deacon who had a bit part in the movie. It was, he said, "reality."

Contestants at the Sutton County Junior Livestock Show, Sonora, 1991

Boys at play on the Concho River near downtown San Angelo

By the late 1980s, the black and white melancholy of *The Last Picture Show* evolved into the Technicolor levity of *Texasville*. The main characters were thirty years older and, if anything, more out of sorts. Unchanged, however, was the location, Archer City. Racy Jacy Farrow was back in town, as beautiful and as mysterious as ever and still surrounded by Duane, Sonny, and her other lustful pals. Duane, star of the high school football team, was now millions in debt from his oil patch miscalculations. Sonny was the town's mayor but more than a little drifty. New to town was Duane's wife, who liked wearing T-shirts that said: "If you love something, set it free. If it doesn't return in a month or two, hunt it down and kill it."

The movie, not as critically acclaimed as *Last Picture Show,* was more fun. It opened with Duane sitting in a hot tub shooting a .44 magnum at a new doghouse. The town's social center was the Dairy Queen—not unlike the real thing. There still was an undercurrent of sexual high jinks, but there was more tolerance, or perhaps resignation, to the ways of the world. The book was a page-turner in

Cotton farming, early 1900s. Cotton is Texas's No. 1 cash crop and Texas is the No. 1 cotton-producing state in the nation in most years, thanks mainly to West Texas. Leading cotton-producing counties in the past decade include a West Texas cluster of Gaines, Lubbock, Hale, Terry, and Hockley, with their neighbors not far behind. Even so, cotton is not Texas agriculture's king. That would be cattle, which brings four times the cash receipts of cotton (Texas Almanac, 1998-99).

Archer City for those who could find it—the library's only copy was always checked out—but pulpit-pounding was notably absent. "It's a different era, for one thing," said jewelry store operator Karla Powell. "I think people have changed. I don't know if we are more lenient or more honest."

It was a local pastime to speculate who inspired the characters in McMurtry's fictional chronicles, which became a trilogy in 1999 with the publication of *Duane's Depressed*. The late Bobby Stubbs, a high school classmate of McMurtry, was partly the model for Duane. At a reception in Wichita Falls, McMurtry said his friend was in the book "because I was afraid if I left him out, it would hurt his feelings." Stubbs, who was fifty-three when *Texasville* hit the bookshelves in 1987, agreed with McMurtry that the books were not about Archer City specifically. "I think every little West Texas town fits the mold he wrote about," said Bobby, owner of an oil well servicing company. "A lot of people pretend life's not that way, but it is."

High Plains savior, pivot irrigation system, Lynn County

Well, I'll be damned!

8

Driller Carl Cromwell, 1923, when Santa Rita No. 1 blew in

A real-life character in somebody's novel about West Texas could be Clayton "Aggie" Williams Jr. And that was before he ran for governor and lost, in part, because he made a remark that ended up more famous than his campaign. He met his wife Modesta while guzzling beer and belting out mariachi songs from a table top in one of his favorite honky-tonks. He created "ClayDesta," a stunning office complex in north Midland, featuring imported trees in a soaring indoor atrium. He adopted the maroon-and-white flag of Texas A&M, his alma mater, as a battle symbol. The flag was once hoisted atop an office building in downtown Midland "to kinda tell them all to go to hell," he said. "That was my war cry. A big bank was picking on me . . . and that was my way of giving 'em the finger." Then there was the time downtown Midland awoke to a pink diaper flapping from the flagpole. It signaled the birth of a daughter, the fifth addition to the Williams brood.

He threw himself into the cattle business, the long-distance telephone business, the banking business, or whatever else would keep him busy. But once or twice a year, he would "shut that son-of-a-gun down" at noon and go drink beer with his Midland employees. He would appear in his own phone commercials and invite seven thousand "friends" to cattle sales at his ranch near Alpine, creating as close to a traffic jam as the vast region ever encountered. When author James

Michener emigrated to Austin to create his own spacious novel about Texas, Claytie obliged by showing him the Trans-Pecos from a helicopter. With the intimidating spirit of a bulldog, Claytie rose from a ten-thousand-dollar-a-year insurance peddler to an oil millionaire in a roller coaster quarter-century punctuated by good luck, misfortune, and hard work. He owed big—almost a half billion dollars at one time—and he scored big.

That is, until he parlayed his money, his flamboyance, and a conservative political message into a race for the governor's mansion in Austin. He stormed through the 1990 Republican primary and faced Democrat Ann Richards, who ultimately proved she could out-cliché and out-poll the political outsider from the West. It didn't help when Claytie decided to haul a bunch of reporters to his Big Bend spread for fall roundup. Perturbed that the weather wouldn't cooperate, he issued an unfortunate line about rape. Paraphrased, he said there was nothing to do but sit back and let it happen.

Still rich by the world's standards, Claytie missed out on Austin and slipped off the public's radar.

Clayton Williams of Midland, candidate for Texas Governor, 1990

"Life in Texas is like a giant crap game, a perpetual gamble," said one of the West Texas characters in Michener's *Texas*. "To succeed, you need grit, courage to take the big chance. A hundred men tried to drive cattle up this trail," the character continued. "They failed. Some of us . . . took great chances and we succeeded, big."

Such was the case on a winter day in 1921 when an ornery wildcatter named Frank Pickrell launched an expedition on a railroad flat car carrying his equipment and his workers. Earlier, there had been a fifty-barrel-a-day strike in Mitchell County east of Big Spring, but it attracted scant attention. Pickrell's destination was farther west and south, although conventional wisdom said there was no oil in far West Texas. He stopped fourteen miles outside of Big Lake in the mesquite, cactus, and chaparral of Reagan County and prepared to go cross-country to his target location. That never happened because a water well machine was damaged in unloading. To meet the deadline on his lease, Pickrell drilled right there near the track while a lease partner with a stalled truck drilled elsewhere at the site of his own breakdown. Pickrell's story is repeated in several accounts, including one in a magazine appropriately named *Oil Patch*. "Through the hours of sundown and into darkness, the little band of workmen pushed desperately," the article said. Just before the midnight deadline, "though the rig had not been completely set up, the well was spudded up." In truth, the water well went dry at its first depth, but Pickrell's drilling met the legal requirements of the lease deadline.

By summer, the equipment for the oil well was shipped from Ranger and an eighty-

The Merriman Baptist Church near Ranger became famous for turning down drilling leases for its cemetery during the 1917 Ranger Oil Boom.

Roughnecks on a West Texas oil rig, early 1900s

No wind for a windmill near Odessa, but plenty of oil below

four-foot wooden rig was erected. Pickrell crawled up the rig and sprinkled dry rose petals that were blessed at a special mass for the expedition's New York investors. The well was named Santa Rita No. 1, after the patron saint of the impossible. For two years, drilling continued through the desert rock until there was a modest "show" at a depth of three thousand feet. The next day, May 28, 1923, the wife of the driller heard a hissing sound near their shack—it could have been a rattlesnake. Then, a slender shaft of oil and gas vapors appeared. Santa Rita No. 1 would produce a modest one hundred barrels a day, and its remote location, the heat, the dust, and a drop in oil prices combined to create a giant yawn from the oil moguls of the time. Pickrell was broke and couldn't develop the field further.

Another wildcatter, Mike Benedum, saved the day, promising to drill eight wells to determine the field's potential. After seven failures, the prospects of incredible wealth were indeed slim, but Benedum ordered Santa Rita No. 5 relocated north of the discovery well. It came in at three hundred barrels a day, enough to keep the project going. Then came No. 9, less than a football field's length from the original well. Bam! Five thousand barrels a day. No. 11, completed next, hit for eight thousand barrels.

Although the Santa Rita strikes were remarkable, Benedum would later figure in the discovery of the Permian Basin's second great oilfield. In it was Yates No. 30-A, which would produce more than two hundred thousand barrels a day in 1929. Other mind-boggling discoveries followed, including the Spraberry Trend and the Canyon Reef, and Midland became the "Tall City," the minicapital of the West Texas oil industry.

Pickrell, according to *Oil Patch,* was another story. He sold out for four and a half million in 1920s dollars, "went broke in the Depression, and made a fortune later."

The West Texas oil business is not all J. R. Ewing, even though Midland had more millionaires per capita at one time than any other city in the nation. Some folks who legitimately call themselves oilmen also farm, teach school, run the hardware store, or drive a truck. "The majors couldn't operate like this," a stripper well operator named Carl Schkade told a reporter in the early '70s. "Stripping is pretty much a family deal." He, his wife, and their teenage son were, in effect, an oil company, squeezing an extra barrel or two out of eighty trickling wells near Baird. They were their own drillers, pipefitters, haulers, riggers, welders, and bookkeepers. To pull pipe, Schkade was using a 1946 truck, last licensed in 1956. The pulling unit was a grimy and grunting relic running on a 1934 flathead Ford motor. There were patches on top of patches. "I guess I'd rather be out here on an old spudder trying to find some new production. It's just like a gold hunter, a prospector. You get a kick out of thinking, 'This time I'm gonna hit and make some money.'" And some did. Most didn't.

In *Oil Legends of Fort Worth*, there is an often told story of Captain S. B. "Burk" Burnett, who was advised by the foreman on his enormous West Texas ranch that oil had been discovered. Mindful of the ongoing drought, Burnett complained, "To hell with oil, I need water for my cattle."

A rancher near the desert village of Toyah west of the Pecos was West Texas's first oilman. Two decades before the strike at Santa Rita No. 1, J. D. Leatherman drilled a small well and found oil at 170 feet. According to *Oil Legends*, he used it to lubricate windmills.

Finally, there's the story of the Merriman Baptist Church in Ranger, where wells were drilled on church grounds after the 1917 gusher. The congregation turned down a hundred thousand dollars in lease payments for the church cemetery "because we do not want the graves of pioneers disturbed."

When it gets this bad, you have to hunker down like a jackrabbit in a hail storm and wait for it to pass.

Former Wichita Falls oilman, James G. O'Donohoe, 1998

9

As grand as it was in Ranger in 1917, the West Texas oil business also can be disastrous. Ask Bubba Gravelhauler, a creation of columnist Ken Brodnax of the *Odessa American*. "Oh, it ain't nothing but the ol' oil patch draggin' me down like an anchor again," Bubba said from his familiar perch on a bar stool at the Crawl On Inn as the 1990s drew to a close. True it was, because crude prices hovered precariously near ten dollars a barrel in his region. Crude was forty dollars a barrel in 1981.

Bubba spoke for a lot of West Texans when he read a fictional letter from his pal Randy Roustabout concerning whether the governor should acknowledge protests of low oil prices. A real-life independent named John Bell of Kermit was helping organize the protests. The governor "ain't no bad feller," the letter began, "but he can't act like he cares about us 'cuz it ain't politically popular. He really does like us as long as we stay in our place and don't cause him no trouble. We gotta remember our governor ain't no different from them other politicians. There ain't none of them gonna do nothin' to help us out here."

But Bubba, according to Brodnax, was philosophical. "We like low prices at the pump, but somebody oughta be remindin' all them people what could happen if all that foreign oil dried up and things was so bad out in these parts that we couldn't produce enough to meet the needs. We'd be right back to long lines and no sales at all on some days. And us folks in the patch would be everybody's best friend."

Bubba had good reason to moan. In January 1999, the number of oil and gas rigs operating in the United States had fallen to its lowest level since the official tally had begun more than a half century before. "When it's as low as it is now," said protester Bell to a reporter, "we're a pretty anemic industry." It was reminiscent of other times, but perhaps not even as bad. "In the 1930s, oil went down to ten cents a barrel," said John Pitts, a writer for the *Midland Reporter-Telegram*. "They were hauling in drinking water at a dollar a barrel. They had to sell ten barrels of oil to purchase one barrel of water."

And consider this from an Associated Press story: "East or west, north or south, Texas history is filled with accounts of rich oil discoveries, boomtowns, grizzled wildcatters, instant millionaires. But the romance is fading. Independents are pulling out. Majors are exploring elsewhere. Related industries are dying." The date: October 25, 1970.

A Wichita Falls oil man named L. H. McCullough said at the time, "Every day I look for a place to drill; I don't give up . . . I got hope. The only thing I can see wrong with the independent oil man is that he might not have hope." A unidentified colleague had more to say: "The Eastern politicians don't give a damn what Texas gets for its oil . . . Let's throw away the slingshot and get a .30-.30 rifle. If we don't fight for a price increase, we're not going to get it."

It was Ed Thompson's turn for a postmortem during a 1983 fallout. He was the hired honcho of the Permian Basin Petroleum Association. Noting that the domestic oil companies paid fifty-seven billion dollars in taxes, he said, "Until we can get the government out of the oil business, along with the Arabs and OPEC, we're going to continue to have problems."

Actually, 1983 was relatively blissful. Midland was simply overbuilt because the betting was for oil to go to fifty or even sixty dollars a barrel. "They crapped out," said Thompson in the days when oil went from forty dollars a barrel to under thirty. Three years later, prices were half that. Promoters were joking that U-Haul and the Federal Insurance Deposit Corporation would be the only exhibitors to show up at the Permian Basin Oil Show in Odessa. They weren't, by the way. The huge turnout spoke volumes about West Texas's propensity for optimism or for hell-raising. Or both.

The most bizarre boom and bust of the 1980s was the so-called white oil phenomenon in the Texas Panhandle. Because old oil and gas prices were regulated, an ingenious promoter or two got the bright idea to refrigerate the gas coming out of the ground, making it viscous enough to be defined as new oil. Refrigeration units sold like nickel longnecks until court challenges and another round of price plunges conspired to end the white oil era.

It was partly the bust of the 1980s that left West Texas mostly bereft of homegrown

Pump jack, work horse for West Texas crude

banks. And the new out-of-state owners were not as open-minded about gambling on the wildcatters' or anybody else's chances for striking what was left of West Texas's reserves. It was a reminder of another passage in Michener's *Texas* about a fictional West Texas banker in the 1880s named Weatherby. The unpopular Weatherby was trying to foreclose on a farmer who had scratched out a frontier horse business on the vast prairie beneath the Caprock. "Why does thee say a money-grubber like Weatherby is necessary?" the farmer asked a cattleman acquaintance. "Because he's the agency that punishes us when our gambles turn sour," was the response. "You escaped him this time, but don't tempt him again, because if Texas is bountiful in rewarding gamblers, it's remorseless in punishing those who stumble."

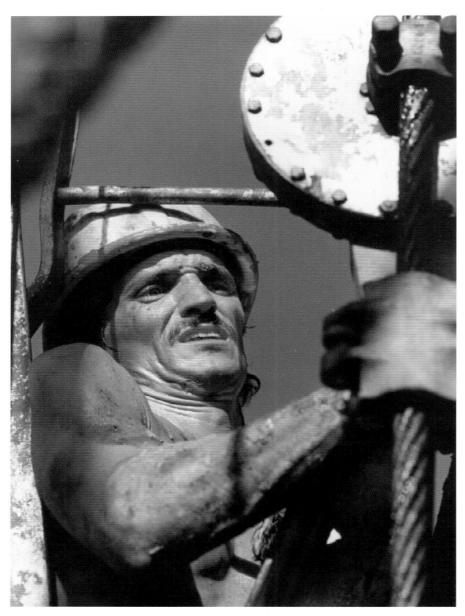

Modern day roughneck Ben Colgan, on rig near Cisco. The work's still hard, dirty, and hot.

To the unpracticed eye, a West Texas pasture is bewildering brown, especially to a visitor used to deep-green lushness.

A. C. Greene, *A Personal Country*

10

A century and a half ago, an Army explorer stumbled onto a hauntingly remote and desolate chunk of Texas prairie and was not much impressed. W. B. Parker branded the hills and plains "inhospitable" and declared, "Destitute of soil, timber, water, game, and everything else that can sustain or make life tolerable, they must remain as they are, uninhabited and uninhabitable." He vowed never to return, except in memory, "and then in reminiscences too painful far to be pleasant."

A giant, jagged rectangle between the skyscrapers of Dallas to the east and the fertile High Plains of Lubbock to the west, the land Parker visited was eventually settled but rarely boomed. Bypassed by major highways and only fitfully romanced by King Cotton or Big Oil, it remains today a region with little population or prosperity and even less political clout. With no name or identity of its own, it often is overlooked or ignored, even by other Texans. "We're really kind of stepchildren here," Micky Parker, the librarian in Jayton once said.

So where is "here"?

Certainly it is well west of Fort Worth and north of Interstate 20. It's also south of the Red River and just to the east of the famous Caprock. By circumstance, not choice, it is an ill-defined territory, relentlessly raw and decorated by hardscrabble farms and ranches and small and struggling towns. To be sure, there are more inhospitable and less populous areas of West Texas, such as Big Bend, the Permian Basin, or even the Badlands west of the Pecos. But those places compensate. The Big Bend has mystique, beauty, and a national park. The Permian has deep, rich oil fields. And the Badlands have history and Hollywood.

A true map of "here" probably would include all or large parts of Dickens, King, Knox, Kent, Stonewall, Fisher, Foard, Cottle, and Motley counties and bits and pieces of Scurry, Jones, Garza, Haskell, and Borden. That's roughly eighty-five hundred square miles, an area larger than the whole of Rhode Island, Delaware, and Connecticut. The largest town is Hamlin, whose population never reached 3,000 in the 1990s. Most are under a thousand.

In all, less than twenty-five thousand people live in this phantom region within a region, many on small farms and larger ranches where the earth yields too few crops and a relative trickle of Texas crude. There is no Alamo, Astrodome, or Cotton Bowl. No daily newspapers, television stations or state universities. The smallest high schools, unable

Native prairie grasses near Benjamin

to field eleven players, play six-man football, sometimes in front of an audience of pickups. In other towns, schools are long closed. Jobs are scarce, health care is erratic, and the population is aging and declining. The weather is hot or blue-norther cold. A dusty wind blows when it doesn't rain, which is most of the time.

So what does the citizenry say of this geographic nonentity? Drugs and crime are pretty much nil, the people are close and caring, and, most of all, it's a great place to raise kids.

Texas's official state photographer, Wyman Meinzer, lives in Benjamin, the Knox County seat. "My best pictures are taken thirty miles from home," he says.

"It's God's country," a resident of Spur named Janelle Barry once insisted. Her hometown comes about as close as any to this region's quasi-capital.

Native son Jim Corder traveled the land he called "the Big Empty" as a child, and he retraced his steps as an adult. But even he couldn't pinpoint the boundaries of his province. "It just doesn't have any identity, except in the minds of the people who live there," he told a reporter.

Corder figured W. B. Parker and his expedition leader, U.S. Army Captain Randolph Marcy, flirted with his homeland when they ventured many years ago into what is now King County. As quoted by Corder, Marcy was even less impressed with the region than Parker. "It is, in almost every respect, the most uninteresting and forbidding land I have ever visited," the commander sniffed. He spoke harshly of its "barren parsimonious soil" and said, "I question if the next century will see it populated by civilized men." Marcy added this churlish note: "Even the Indians shun this country . . . so that the bears are left in undisturbed possession."

Rule, Texas, 1994—Prevailing south winds lash the gnarled mesquite trees, and surly gray clouds hint of a rare summer rain as a visitor arrives at the southeastern edge of Jim Corder's cosmos. Many of Rule's 783 residents are sipping coffee at Casey's Country Kitchen. The playground at Slim Sorrells Park is as empty as the Western Winds Motel and the Rule Memorial Museum, which is open by appointment only. On the main drag, a mural memorializes the shuttered Rule Theater. It depicts a young boy at the ticket window with a balloon-toting girl at his side. The mural's double feature: *The Three*

Stooges and *Mutiny on the Bounty.* Although its best years may be past, Rule still has a drive-in movie, open weekends from April until it gets cold.

On the deserted main street, at Primitives and Collectibles, there is an Open sign, a locked door, and this note: "If you would like to look—Go to Allsups and call 997-2324. I'll be there in five minutes and please do not feel obligated to buy. Thanks, Maxine." Outside of Rule, there are mossy stock tanks and idle oil pumps, a modern brick home with cattle grazing in the yard, a wildly spinning windmill, and a few cultivated fields.

Across the Double Mountain Fork of the Brazos is a German settlement once named Brandenburg but for patriotic purposes renamed Old Glory in 1918. An American flag flutters in the center of what is now little more than a shell town. Its school shut down eight years ago, the grocery–service station

Charlene Webb and her yard of collectibles in Aspermont, Stonewall County

Postmaster Lisbon Letz lowers the flag in Old Glory, Stonewall County.

more recently. "Right now, I'm the only fella here," drawls Lisbon Letz, the Old Glory postmaster for thirty-six years. "Time's starting to pass pretty quick now."

Aspermont, population 1,214, is the home of the Aspermont Hornets and Hornet Pride and the county seat of Stonewall County, named for Confederate General T. J. "Stonewall" Jackson. A landmark bank looks as if its last visitors, if not Stonewall and the troops, were Bonnie and Clyde. The Ace Motel offers rooms for "$17 and up." Nearby is a cheerful home surrounded by surely the strangest collectibles in all of West Texas, if not the world. Bordered by a fence of bedsprings and wrought iron bedposts, the treasures include old farm machinery, decorative rocks and stones, wagon wheels, nail barrels,

driftwood, milk cans, and even a faux yellow duck and ducklings.

On the highway is the Dairy Queen—a Big Empty staple—with three weathered customers in the uniform of the day: low-slung jeans, big-buckled belts, scruffy cowboy boots, and soiled straw western hats. Like most West Texans, they're as friendly as beagle pups.

Down the road is Swenson, so-named for the once great Swenson ranching empire but now a ghost town, with only traces of its noble past. The most forlorn remnant is a red brick bank, founded in 1911. The hot Texas sun peers through gaping holes in the roof, and, over the doorway, an awning of metal and wood hangs like something long dead. Cactus plants keep lonely vigil at the open entrance. Fat cattle adorned with the famous

Nature creates a pattern in red clay.

SMS brand once roamed ranches in central, west, and northwest Texas, and few natives know the country better than Gene Swenson of Stamford. "There's a lot of this damn land that the only thing you can do is run a cow on it," he says. "Basically, this is ranch country." Recalling attempts to cultivate this rugged land, he smiles ruefully. "In my opinion, some of it was plowed up that shouldn't have been."

The walls of the shuttered Barfoot Hotel in Jayton are cracked and the paint has peeled, but a twisted oak tree still provides shade for the grand old lady. The weekly *Jayton Chronicle* is closed as well, even though the town has fared better than most. Mobil Oil and the highway department are active employers, and there is a Chevrolet dealership. Jayton also is the county seat—but that was not always so. According to one juicy tale, cattle trucks whisked the county records from the original courthouse in Clairemont and then a fire mysteriously destroyed the building. The records surfaced in Jayton, and so did a new courthouse.

"That makes a good story," laughs librarian Micky Parker, "but cattle trucks didn't back up there and move the records at night." Furthermore, she says, an electrical fire during a sandstorm in the drought-ridden 1950s demolished the Clairemont courthouse.

There is no mystery about the Jayton school system, which is first class. "When my brother played football at Jayton," Jim Corder wrote, "I remember watching the principal draw off the yard markers in the dirt with a hoe." Ironically, Jayton's superb educational system became threatened by the state's so-called Robin Hood school finance plan, which funnels tax money from rich to poor districts. As a school official once explained: "Our people are very poor. We just happen to have a pool of oil in the center of the county."

A downtown historical marker reveals that the Double Mountain Salt Works was located along the Brazos River on the "Indian-

The Double Mountains in Stonewall County. There once was a community called Double Mountain nearby, but like a lot of communities across the plains, it's gone now.

infested frontier" and was the northernmost business in Confederate Texas. Salt was scarce during the Civil War but was essential to cure meat and hides for leather, season food, and feed workhorses, army draft mules and cavalry horses. West of town, toward Clairemont, salt crystals still sparkle in a dry river bed.

Knox City, population 1,440, has a friendly catfish and chicken fried steak place called Debbie's, but across the street the Oil Patch Cafe is closed and abandoned. The golf course looks prosperous, and the main street is shaded by sycamores, pecans, mesquites, and mimosas. A church marquee captures the flavor of this entire region: Like Life, Few Gardens Have Only Flowers.

On Ranch Road 222, the terrain turns hilly and rocky, but an oasis of sorts, the Chaparral, appears out of nowhere to offer wine, beer, and liquor. It is one of few such liquid outposts. Purple wildflowers, defying all odds, sprout along the road, and a lonely cow is wedged under a shade tree in a far-away field. The road feeds into U.S. 82 and, after crossing the South Wichita River, which is bone dry in the summer, leads into Guthrie, past the King County Courthouse and up to the headquarters of the 6666. The *Texas Almanac* puts the county population at 367, not quite half of it in Guthrie, and says income is mostly from ranching and minerals. "You've found a good place to get lost," chuckles county employee and part-time librarian Karen Pettiet, who has lived here almost all of her forty years.

Only 322 people call Dickens, Texas, their home, but they have the essentials of all West Texas towns: a Church of Christ, a Baptist church, and a cemetery. The drive-in is history, so Dickens has a youth-oriented video business operating out of a house. A sign alerts teens to the Thursday night movie. They bring quilts, pillows, candy, and soft drinks and flop down in front of a television screen equipped with a VCR. "We've got twenty-five kids in town and we've been

having about thirty show up," notes proprietor Mike Porter. "So we think it's a success."

In neighboring Spur, a garbage company once announced in the weekly paper that trash would not be picked up as scheduled because of a holiday. It added, "The whole town will be picked up on Tuesday."

The historic Mackenzie Trail passes between Dickens and Spur near a spot known as Soldier Mound. More than a century ago, thousands of settlers followed the trail westward, settling along its path. In 1874, Colonel Ranald Mackenzie led U.S. Army troops up the trail to Palo Duro Canyon and a decisive battle with the Comanche and Kiowa. The army won.

Today, Spur has thirteen hundred people, a ranching legacy, a Hot Iron Cafe, a Dixie Dog, and a wrought iron sign that proclaims this is "A great place to live." One who agrees is Janelle Barry. "I was born here and liked it well enough to come back when my husband retired." Her birthplace suffers identity problems, she admits. Her friends in Fort Worth would ask her what's it close to? Her answer: "It's not close to anything."

James Corder thought it was close to God. In his book, he insisted God's residing place is the Double Mountains. He acknowledged that the mountains could be mistaken for two hills but, regardless, they lie in Stonewall County and are visible for miles in any direction.

Along U.S. 380 near the turnoff to Peacock, the Double Mountains appear off to the left and tantalizingly close. FM 2211 passes through the tiny town but the lone sign of life is a mockingbird in a dead tree outside a tin-topped tabernacle, now the Peacock Community Center. A sign stenciled on the door of a small, white building announces that "The King is coming soon. Get ready."

Go outside, build up a fire, and broil me a steak. Build it under my window, close to the house, so I can smell it cooking.

Dying cowman Walter Cochran of Midland to his friend, historian J. Evetts Haley

11

If the Chisholm Trail lives on, it should be called the Cholesterol Trail.

There's no escaping Cattlemen's in the Fort Worth Stockyards, where grainy photographs honor champion bovines of the past. Or the Bar-L in Wichita Falls, where present-day carhops serve cold red-draws with ribs that sizzle. For the price of a hot dog in Chicago, there's Monkey's brisket in Borger, Sally's green chile burgers in Pecos, Sarah's enchiladas in Fort Stockton, and Allen's family-style fried chicken in Sweetwater.

Fried catfish may be a crown prince, but steak's still king—whether it's a chicken-fried platter at Possum Hollow on Possum Kingdom Lake, a ribeye at Joe Allen's in Abilene, a peppered sirloin at the 50-Yard Line in Lubbock, or a KC strip at Perini's Steak Ranch in Buffalo Gap.

Figure this: the owner of Perini's, and his cookware, were escorted to Japan to demonstrate his West Texas grilling expertise. Don't worry, his foreign friends did not purloin the pump jack in Perini's gravel parking lot or steal the ambiance of his tree-shaded courtyard.

The taste in West Texas beef emporiums is in fact often exquisite and the price is usually right, and few are more famous than yesteryear's Lowake Inn northeast of San Angelo. Folks from hundreds of miles around would drive or even fly into the private airstrip near the barnlike inn to guzzle frosty mugs of beer and consume platters of grilled steaks swimming in natural juices and enhanced by mounds of freshly cut french fries. The airstrip and the inn are closed now, but the Lowake Steak House up the road provides many fond memories and a performance not unlike classical music.

The cook, Helen Fisher, "turns toward her grill and waves a spatula like a conductor uses a baton," observed Rick Smith of the *San Angelo Standard-Times* in 1992. "Her steakhouse symphony begins. First movement: Gravy. Half a gallon of milk flows into a heavy pan. She pours in a scoop of flour, then another, then another. Stir–stir–stir–stir–stir . . ." Helen, then eighty-two, had been behind that stove since middle age, when a hail storm flattened her family's farm in nearby Rowena. "Someday I'll probably be too old to do this," she said. "But not today, though."

Lowake's legacy lives on in another West Texas oasis or two. They drive from Brownwood in droves for Caroline's in Coleman (1) because the T-bones are thumbs-up and, (2) because Caroline's is wet.

Movie stars have found their way to Fort Griffin General Merchandise near Albany for an aged fourteen-ounce filet under twenty bucks. Fort Griffin's proprietors, the Esfandiary brothers, were stranded in West Texas as members of the Iranian air force when the Shah was ousted in their homeland. To obtain a loan for a restaurant, they had to promise to make chicken fried steak. Money in hand, they asked each other, "What's that?"

The Country Barn in Amarillo has barbecue as well as steaks, and there is a vintage '57 Impala convertible in the bar to boot. For a peppered plateful of top sirloin, there's Zentner's and Zentner's Daughter in San Angelo and Abilene. But the best deal in West Texas may be not in Texas, but just over the border from El Paso in New Mexico at Billy Crews steak house, where there's famed Silver Oak cabernet for under seventy dollars a bottle—half the price of those come-lately cow palaces in Big D or Houston.

Arbitration is required when it comes to favorite West Texas barbecue joints. There's double meat at Dyer's in Pampa, brisket and ice-rimmed mugs of beer at Angelo's in Fort Worth, and take-out at Big John's in Big Spring. (Big John's menu is on a paper sack, and fly swatters are free.) If you believe Llano at least straddles West Texas, you can include Cooper's pit-smoked pork chop. Also the sirloin, the ribs, the goat, and the chicken, and you're too full to cross the finish line.

For sheer heft, there's the Big Texan Steak Ranch on Interstate 40 near Amarillo, which ballyhoos a free seventy-two-ounce chunk of beef for anyone who can eat it in an hour. Ben Heiple of Pampa showed up in 1998 with Taboo the tiger, who wolfed down the monster in ninety seconds. "For dessert, they gave him a second one," says Heiple, grinning. "They were really nice people."

The best description of a West Texas meal can be found in a 1994 biography of Watt Matthews of Lambshead Ranch by Lawrence Clayton, who experienced the feast firsthand. "Lunch included thick slabs of sirloin steak cooked as a pot roast with onions, large chunks of deep-fried potatoes, green beans seasoned with bacon drippings, lettuce and tomatoes, and a marvelous cherry cobbler . . . Presiding over the meal and visiting with the hands was Watt himself."

And while Oprah Winfrey fought her beef defamation court battle in the Texas Panhandle, no one seemed too intimidated by all that talk of mad cow disease. At the Lone Star Bar & Grill, a waitress made it clear the only items on the menu were beef, adding with a flourish: "We serve only mad cows—REALLY mad cows." They also peddled caps and shirts with inscriptions proclaiming, "The only mad cow in Texas is Oprah."

The Oprah show roared into Amarillo in January 1998 because an aggravated bunch of Panhandle cattle feeders were eager to test Texas's new veggie libel law. They claimed Oprah's mad cow comments caused a drop in prices, and they wanted America's richest female entertainer to pay.

They didn't anticipate Oprah's local popularity or the intransigence of another female, "Maximum" Mary Lou Robinson of the U.S. District Court. When it was over, the cattle feeders lost, but not before making the Texas-flavored tapings of "The Oprah Winfrey Show" the hottest ticket in town. There were bumper stickers and buttons proclaiming "Amarillo loves Oprah." The

Sally's North Side Café in Pecos has a grocery on one side and dining room on the other. The cash register is in the middle.

Dinner time at Perini's Steak Ranch, Buffalo Gap

Eat a 72-ounce sirloin in an hour and you don't pay at the Big Texan in Amarillo.

chamber of commerce president misspoke early about Oprah not being welcome and then spent two embarrassing weeks backtracking. Calls for tickets to her show were so heavy one day they overloaded the phone company's circuitry and disrupted service citywide. "Generally speaking," said lawyer Dee Miller, "even people in the cattle industry have been very positive to her." This was in a town where steak and barbecue emporiums proliferate with names like Black Angus, Beef Rigger, Hoffbrau, Cattleman's, Cattle Call, and Fat-Boys, in addition to the "world famous" Big Texan. That wasn't lost on the horde of network reporters covering the trial. Nor was the huge mural at the courthouse

that depicted cowboys herding cattle on a railroad box car.

Maximum Mary Lou first decided that Oprah couldn't have libeled a hamburger, making the cattle feeders try their suit as simple business disparagement. A jury did the rest. And, as an aside, the judge even muzzled the Panhandle Mouth that Roared. Ol' Stanley Marsh, never at a loss for comment about Amarillo courthouse capers, was a limited partner in one of the cattle companies suing Oprah and therefore fell under the judge's gag order. "This is awful. Just terrible," said Stanley. "I don't know a Hereford from a heifer."

In truth, much cowboy work was—and is—bone hard, deadly boring, and discouragingly repetitious. Mending fences, kicking salt blocks out of truck beds, shoeing horses, working the cranks, handles, pulleys, chains, and gates of squeeze chutes against panicky critters who wish to be neither branded, castrated, vaccinated, or dehorned . . .

Larry L. King, "Vanishing Texas," *Texas Monthly,* 1990

12

West Texas without cowboys? Better to think of chicken fried steak without cream gravy. Cowboys still work the JA, the Matador, the Waggoner, the Pitchfork, and scores of other giant spreads. The mystique and the heritage stay alive at the Ranch Roundup in Wichita Falls, the XIT Rodeo & Reunion in Dalhart, the Boys Ranch Rodeo on Labor Day weekend, and a corral full of other smaller competitions. The town of Stamford swells to three times its size in early July with the Texas Cowboy Reunion, called the world's greatest amateur rodeo. The granddaddy of them all—or at least it claims to be—is the West of Pecos Rodeo in the far West Texas town of Pecos. With trucks whining on the nearby interstate highway and temperatures close to 100 degrees, professional cowboys do

Pecos has a historic rodeo, but it's known more for cantaloupes than cattle.

Cowboy lassoes a horse from a remuda on a West Texas ranch, circa 1950.

what their amateur predecessors did on July 4 more than a century ago—rope and ride horses, chase steers, and argue about who's the best.

Even so, the West Texas cowboy's storied life is disappearing—lost to the cattle trucks that replaced the cattle drive, to the feedlots that fatten the stock more efficiently than the range and to the all-terrain vehicles and helicopters that have succeeded the horse and saddle. Lost to the soft life of the town, the cozy seat of an air-conditioned pickup. And probably for good reason. "When I see a ranch house, I think of hard work and loneliness," Larry L. King once wrote.

One cowboy who stayed in the saddle was Tom Blasingame, who was 18 when he began punching cows on the JA in 1916. The end came in Palo Duro Canyon in December 1989, as described by a Western writer from Midland, Patrick Dearen, in *The Last of the Old-Time Cowboys:*

Alone now, with nothing but crow's feet and sagging shoulders to betray the passage of years, Blasingame turned his horse away from the primitive line shack near Campbell Creek and rode into a sprawling country fit for a cowboy. He broke trail through the brush unaware of the burden he shouldered, for he was the last remnant of the last-of-a-breed men who had cowboyed before mechanization . . .

Prowling the breaks near Bull Run Creek, a tributary of the Big Red, he evidently realized he was in trouble. Dismounting, he stretched out on his back in the Palo Duro grass at the hooves of his horse. With feet firm in his boots, he folded his arms across his chest, closed his eyes to the fading sun of the Old West, and died the way a cowboy should.

Cowboy Jimmy Byrd takes a breather during a branding session at the Waggoner Ranch, 1986. Founded in 1849 and headquartered in Vernon, its 520,000 acres penetrate six West Texas counties. But its distinction of being Texas's largest ranch under one fence has been threatened in the 1990s by family disputes.

There must have been a lot of rain that winter, for the clover was abundant. It would be a good year for the cattle herds.

Larry McMurtry, *Streets of Laredo*, describing the landscape en route to Charles Goodnight's ranch in the Texas Panhandle.

"Even while the cowman was opposed to the cowman over fences," historian T. R. Fehrenbach wrote in *Lone Star*, "the intrusion of the hoeman went on." Nowhere was the conflict more prevalent than the High Plains of West Texas, and the loss of the open range was inevitable. Even though success was not guaranteed in a harsh climate, public policy and dwindling opportunities in the Midwest encouraged the family farmer. Foreign investors also sold off huge tracts of ranchland for farming—the XIT and the Matador among them. Family feuds, lack of heirs, drought, land speculation, or land too worthless to support a cow all contributed to the disappearing culture of the cowboy, although, ironically, cattle sales represent more than half the agricultural revenue in nearly all of Texas's 254 counties. Here's the tell-tale statistic: In the mid-1990s, feedlots with one thousand head or more of cattle accounted for more than 99 per cent of the cattle fed in Texas. Most are concentrated in the South Plains and Panhandle.

Cooling off, SMS Ranch, Bob Criswell and Magnus "Swede" Swenson,1950s

Branding cattle, early 1900s

Stag dance, Spur Ranch, circa 1900. At the turn of the century, some ranches had few or no female residents.

The chuck wagon, invention of Charles Goodnight, on the Matador Ranch, early 1900s

Farmer plows across an old cattle trail on the West Texas plains, early 1900s. No cattle would walk that trail again.

Large ranches were subdivided in the early 1900s and offered as relatively inexpensive farmland. Salesmen met prospective buyers from the Midwest at the train.

I n Texas more than any other place in the world, the house of the toiler, or the aggressive farmer in his castle, and though he live or die, succeed or fail, the faithful woman who has worked with him, and the tiny baby in her arms, will be defended and nourished by strong laws which were made and enforced in their behalf.

Sales pitch for prospective wives to settle in Texas, quoted in "The Last of the Great Prairie Farming Lands," issued by the South and West Land Company, 1906.

We had a two-day meeting, Saturday and Sunday, and I want to tell you, the Word of God sunk deep.

Rancher John Zack Means, about the first Bloys Camp Meeting, from *Circuit Riders of the Big Bend,* by W. D. Smithers

13

West Texans do not live by brisket alone, although some try. In fact, there's a barbecue joint with a spiritual twist in Abilene, which, with three church colleges, is pretty much unchallenged as the buckle on the regional Bible Belt. At Harold's, Harold himself is known to serenade customers with lunchtime hymns.

But even Abilenians didn't deserve the House of Yahweh. According to *Texas Monthly,* the religious sect believed Satan is a woman, the Pope was her puppet, and the world would end in a couple of years. The group's "pastor and overseer" was identified as a former Abilene cop who called himself Yisrayl Hawkins, but was known as Buffalo Bill when he sang with a rockabilly band called the Whippoorwills. "Weird don't describe them," said an Abilene reporter, even though the House had its own Internet web site by 1999.

In the 1970s, the Children of God settled near Thurber for a spell, and the followers of David Terrell overran the area near Bangs and Coleman until allegations of tax evasion eroded Brother Terrell's appeal. More recently, it was revealed that the Heaven's Gate guru, Marshall Herff Applewhite, was from Spur.

In the 1960s, the dean of women at one of the Abilene's church schools fretted openly about the carnal concerns of students jamming into cars to go to Sunday school. She decreed that boys place Sunday newspapers in their laps if girls intended to sit there.

Clarendon has its own religious roots and a century-old nickname: "Saint's Roost." That's because it was founded by a Methodist preacher as a "sobriety settlement," in contrast to towns that catered to hell-raising for saddle-sore cowpokes.

In 1993, Floydada had evangelist Sammy Rodriguez, who was convinced the Devil was about to usurp his Panhandle town. The Lord instructed Reverend Sammy to take his flock to Florida, but mechanical problems reduced the six-car caravan to just one by the time they reached the Louisiana border. By this time, they were also naked, the Lord having commanded them to surrender all their worldly goods in Galveston. Reverend Sammy's pilgrimage ended when the car crashed through a fence at the baseball park in Vinton, Louisiana. Sammy and his nineteen followers, still unclothed, tumbled out, miraculously unhurt.

In 1998, a Baptist minister in Wichita Falls denounced a pair of public library books, *Heather Has Two Mommies* and *Daddy's Roommate*, that depict homosexual parents. The campaign triggered a controversy that polarized the city, and compelled the library to obtain more copies to keep up with the newfound demand.

Such excess surely would tickle Marj Carpenter, a tough, salty, scotch-sipping ex-newspaper reporter from Big Spring and, strangely, the region's most famous contemporary Christian. Unlikely as it seemed to former colleagues, Marj served as moderator of the entire Presbyterian Church U.S.A. for a year and traveled the globe with a missionary's zeal. Everyone loved her.

"Whirlwind for the Lord," flashed a headline about Marj Carpenter, who partied with American presidents, rafted the Rio Grande with Lady Bird, and roared through the West Texas skies with the famous Air Force Thunderbirds. "She will look danger in the eye and not blink," said one church leader.

At age sixty-nine, this merry messiah launched a global tour of Presbyterian outposts, insisting "a lot of people are out there in the dark and cold waiting for the church to come to them." She wasn't much for fractious church politics that focused on sexual orientation and abortion. She was asked her stance on the latter when she was elected church moderator. "I've never had an abortion and I'm sure none of these other candidates have, either," Marj said, referring to two male opponents.

The only sibling in her family to reach adulthood, she helped a husband through college by teaching high school choir and then descended on the far West Texas town of Pecos just as the empire of Billie Sol Estes started to rot. She landed a job at the semi-weekly *Pecos Independent and Enterprise,* a frequent critic of Billie Sol.

Marj's paper would be pivotal in exposing Estes—the editor won a Pulitzer Prize for doing so—but not before competition turned ugly between the *Independent* and Billie Sol's startup newspaper. Someone put an old gray snake in Marj's car and a sign on the steering wheel that said: "This could have been a rattlesnake." She boxed up the serpent and dumped it in the yard of the person she suspected put it in her car. More worrisome was the brick that someone tossed through her son's bedroom window or the night someone set the *Independent* ablaze. Then, almost like the test of Job, her husband killed himself while cleaning a shotgun and she lost her job.

Undaunted, she found her way to Big Spring and another newspaper job with Joe Pickle, a West Texas press institution himself. He hired her, almost fired her, and later said, "She's one of a kind."

Bangs, Texas, 1974—Darkness had not fallen when the Prophet arrived, chauffeured along a dusty road to a secluded spot behind a large green tent. He stepped from the Mercedes sedan and disappeared into a trailer house. Inside the wind-whipped tent, his followers were assembling, some praying silently. Most of the men wore work clothes and the women long dresses, responding to the Prophet's distaste for "men looking like women and women looking like men."

The Prophet's followers were arriving daily in growing numbers. They lived in tents, trailer homes, and abandoned farm houses, swelling the public school systems. "I've seen them give TV sets, the shirt off their back, live hogs, watches, and stuff," said one man whose wife joined the migration. "They take up the collection in an old lard bucket."

Brown County Sheriff Danny Neal was plainly worried. Two children died after their

Giant Crosses of Our Lord Jesus Christ, Groom

parents declined to seek medical treatment. The father of one said, "I believe it was the will of God, and if he wanted her to die, it don't make no difference if I took her to five hundred doctors."

The Prophet, whose real name was David Terrell, was rumored to live in a luxury bus. He sometimes flew a leased Aero Commander turboprop. An employee of the Lone Star Motel and Trailer Court in Waco said he stayed there for nine months in an Airstream trailer. There were other colonies somewhere in South Carolina, Tennessee, Alabama, and possibly Arkansas. Followers claimed he healed the blind, deaf, mute, crippled, and cancerous and, in one instance, raised the dead. He once fasted, they said, for ten months.

The Prophet appeared in a jacket and blue shirt without a tie. He picked up a guitar and sang a half-dozen songs, pausing to ask, "Don't you love Him?" His sermon targeted dry-eyed preachers, false prophets, honky-tonks, and sin-filled cities. God is not dead, he said, just the church. There was much talk of earthquakes, famine, crop failures, food shortages, energy shortages, war and scandals in government. "We know a judgment's coming on this generation," he shouted, pacing back and forth. With the x-ray eyes he said God gave him, he focused on perhaps three dozen members of the audience for the healing to begin. This, however, was not a night for the blind or crippled. Mostly, female disorders, back pains, nervous stomachs, and several unspecified ailments were addressed.

A chorus of hallelujahs accompanied each "miracle." A young man rolled on the dirt floor. The Prophet hopped wildly across the stage, sometimes wiggling in delight. He

83

threw a handkerchief wet with sweat to the congregation, then another, and then another. There was pandemonium when many worshipers rushed the stage for his "prayer cloths." Then came the appeal to support the Prophet's work. One follower, short on cash, gave a goldfish, complete with bowl. When the offering was finished, the Prophet summoned the flock to the foot of the stage and, on cue, an associate led the closing prayer. While heads were bowed, the Prophet slipped off stage, collection bucket in hand, out the rear of the tent, and into the waiting Mercedes, vanishing into the West Texas night. So, in years to come, would his followers.

It would never be mistaken for the architecturally wondrous St. Paul's Cathedral in London, but modest St. Paul's in the Panhandle town of Kress has its own unique history. "A lot of work has gone into this place," said parishioner Joe Maldonado of St. Paul's construction, "but not a penny has been spent by anybody."

A closely knit group of about thirty mostly Hispanic families wanted a church in their own community, even if their priest split time on a twentieth-century circuit ride among Kress, Silverton, and Tulia. Problem was, there was no building. Then someone spotted a vacant structure in downtown Plainview made of rock. Once a funeral home, it also had been a law office, apartments, and even a beauty parlor. Maldonado, who worked at an auto parts store, went to the owner, the *Plainview Daily Herald,* to inquire.

The paper's publisher, James Thomas, said the building wasn't for sale. Crestfallen, Maldonado asked why. "Because we're going to donate it to you," Thomas said. On Sundays thereafter, the parishioners tore down

the building stone by stone and hauled it to Kress, mostly by pickup. The congregation also did the plumbing, the electrical work, and the painting.

After obtaining the building from the *Herald,* the congregation submitted names for the church to the bishop in Amarillo. He picked "St. Paul's." Three months later, workers discovered an August 1936 calendar page in the attic. It bore a painting of the apostle Paul.

Although little known, the first "Law West of the Pecos" was not Judge Roy Bean, but Gaspar Castano de Sosa, the leader of a Spanish expedition. So says *Pioneer Jewish Texans,* a book about Jewish contributions to Texas. Castano entered Texas at what is now Del Rio in 1590 and led his party beyond the Pecos River into present-day New Mexico. He was "rugged as Coronado, as idealistic and sometimes as comic as Don Quixote."

Author Natalie Ornish describes other Jewish settlers who left an imprint on West Texas. David Spangler Kaufman, the first Texan to be seated in the U.S. Congress, helped forge the compromise for Texas's western boundaries after first arguing they should have stretched to Wyoming.

Two brothers, Mayer and Soloman Halff, drove cattle on the Chisholm Trail, and the family's ranchlands encompassed more than six million acres before the advent of barbed wire. Their ranches in West Texas included the Circle Dot near Marathon, the Quien Sabe near Midland, and the J.M. along the Pecos River. An employee once wrote that Mayer Halff "practiced what he preached, and made a fortune in the land that Charles Goodnight called 'the graveyard of a cowman's hopes' along the Rio Pecos and Rio Grande."

There were others, like German immigrant Olga Kohlberg, who helped establish

Baptisms at Buffalo Springs, early 1900s

Texas's first kindergarten in El Paso in 1884, and Abraham Luskey, a Russian cobbler, whose Fort Worth boot shop was the start of a western wear store chain extending from Abilene to Odessa to Lubbock. And finally, Haymon Krupp, who came to El Paso from Lithuania and became a dry goods clerk. He eventually owned his own store and had a standing offer to the coal companies to supply fuel to the poor at his expense.

But that was not the end of the story. Krupp was, in fact, the lease partner of Frank Pickrell and devised the original stock offering for wildcatting on state lands dedicated to the University of Texas. Although he isn't mentioned in every account, Krupp was trudging through the same desert as his partner when Pickrell dug the first hole. That, of course, led to the drilling of Santa Rita No. 1 and the phenomenal West Texas gushers of the Permian Basin that followed.

Throw the ball, throw the ball!

14

Texas Christian football coach Dutch Meyer, instructing his quarterback, Sammy Baugh

A half-century or more ago, golfer Hoolie White made a hole-in-one at the No. 6 hole on the Anson municipal course. Did it again in 1997, at age ninety-one. "The women in town have been all over him since the news came out," said fellow golfer Jeep Spurgin.

West Texans are sports crazy, which was demonstrated more recently by the rousing red-carpet welcome of the Dallas Cowboys to their new summer camp at Wichita Falls. Maybe it's because West Texas has no Cowboys—or any other major professional sports team—of its own. But it does have the Winters Blizzards, the Mojo of Odessa Permian and the only high school team named after a West Texas dust storm, the Amarillo Sandies.

Improbably, minor league hockey gained a West Texas foothold in the 1990s. The teams had exotic names: Odessa Jackalopes, El Paso Buzzards, San Angelo Outlaws, and the Amarillo Rattlers. And then there's Wayland Baptist University, which put Plainview on the sports map in the mid-1950s. The Flying Queens are still the nation's winningest women's basketball program and they also own the sport's longest winning streak, 131 games. Long before gender equity, aviator and alumnus Claude Hutcherson flew the team to road games, hence the name. Claude's son Mike continues the traveling tradition four decades later.

Tiny Vega upheld another West Texas tradition in 1999, winning a girls' basketball state championship in Class A. In all, girls' basketball teams from West Texas have claimed forty percent of the state titles since 1950, the year the first statewide championship was held. Since 1976, it's more than half. Canyon High's girls, whose training begins in the seventh grade, are responsible for two 4A state championships in the '90s. The gym starts filling up two hours before game time. By 1997, Nazareth won thirteen state titles. Only three high schools in the entire United States won more, highlighting West Texas's status as a girls' basketball hotbed. "I think one reason for that is that early on, the small schools had girls' basketball and the big schools didn't," said Marsha Sharp, who grew up in the Panhandle. She's an authority to boot, having coached the Texas Tech Lady Raiders to a women's NCAA basketball championship.

West Texas lays claim to Texas's only men's NCAA basketball championship, too. The remarkable run of Texas Western changed the character of college basketball, as well. The coach, Don Haskins, recruited African-American players from around the country to what is now the University of Texas at El Paso and startled the all-white basketball bluebloods from the University of

Girls' basketball team, Lubbock, 1916

Kentucky. Coach Don is still at courtside piling up wins almost three decades later.

Stamford's Charles Coody was one of Gordon Wood's star quarterbacks but attended Texas Christian on a basketball scholarship and somehow majored in golf, a smart move as it turned out. A Masters champ, he became a millionaire fixture on the PGA senior circuit. Thanks to Coody, Wood also won a state golf championship, despite losing another top player. On the senior trip to New Orleans, one of Coody's teammates returned to the hotel "all beered up," Wood recalled, "and I had to cut him."

Meanwhile, NFL party animal Bobby Layne chose to live his version of the good life in Lubbock. Because most of his adventures were nocturnal, he confessed that he liked his streets "straight and wide."

One sad note from Lubbock: Texas Tech's mascot, a jet black horse named Double T, was killed in a freak sideline accident during a 1994 football game. A committee recommended abolishing the game-day tradition of the mascot's sideline gallops. Instead, the committee was abolished.

The cloud that hung over Odessa High's football team ended on October 26, 1997, when they beat storied Odessa Permian for the first time in thirty-two years. There were twenty thousand fans in the stands for the battle. Defensive end Jeffrey Kupper scored Odessa's first touchdown, scooping up a fumble in one motion and dashing untouched into the end zone. "It's indescribable," said Jeffrey. "I've been watching this stuff since my uncle played."

Odessa High celebrates victory over rival Permian, 1997.

Permian's mystique suffered after the publication of *Friday Night Lights,* a book that depicted coaches as manipulative and tyrannical. But the darkest portrait of West Texas football emerged in *Varsity Blues,* a 1999 movie in the fictional town of West Canaan. West Canaan's coach, actor Jon Voight, threatens to ruin anyone who challenges his authority and forces one seriously injured lineman to play anyway. Obnoxious fans in a football-mad town live vicariously through the teenaged players, who ultimately rebel.

"If that's really what people see when they come down here, they need to check their glasses," said David Baugh, the coach at Snyder High. "I'm not saying that nothing bad ever happens," Big Spring Coach Dwight Butler told an AP reporter. "I'm just surprised that these folks from up north can find out so much about it when I've never seen any of it."

If West Texas didn't have a pro team in reality, leave it to novelist Dan Jenkins to create one. The author of *Semi-Tough* and *Dead Solid Perfect* awarded the Texas High Plains a fictional pro football franchise and launched it on a run for the Super Bowl in his book, *Rude Behavior.*

Kevin Costner's movie character in *Tin Cup* was a West Texas driving range pro, but *Tin Cup*'s high jinks couldn't compare to the real-life rumbles at yesteryear's Odessa Pro-Am. Touring pros and Hollywood stars descended on Odessa for the annual summertime frolic. The highlight was not the scoreboard but the tote board, which gave Vegas-style odds on the golfers.

Stranger still, two Lubbock country clubs discovered oil in the 1980s, leading one golfer to say: "In Lubbock, the country clubs loan money, not vice versa." So why was the president of one club staring glumly into his drink? "We drilled another water well," he said, "and struck oil again."

Historians know the ancient golf courses of Scotland were sometimes six holes, five holes, or whatever before a standard of eighteen was set. To this day, there's an eleven-hole course in Pecos. It's a product of West Texas ingenuity. They flood two fairways at a time to water the grass, keeping the other nine open for play.

At Weeks Park, the municipal course in Wichita Falls, they erected a sign in honor of Ben Crenshaw at the creek spanning the fairway in front of the eighteenth hole. That was where the Masters champ, as a junior golfer, hit what he called "the most incredible shot

. . . in my life." He won the annual Texas-Oklahoma Junior Golf Tournament in 1970 when a booming three-wood headed toward the ditch but somehow managed to roll across a bridge before nestling safely on the other side.

Golf eventually replaced football and calf-roping as Sammy Baugh's favorite pastime. West Texas's most famous quarterback was traveling from his Double Mountain Ranch to play four or five rounds a week, six decades after he competed in "The Game of the First Half Century," TCU versus SMU in 1935.

And who can forget the incredible Bobby Morrow, age twenty, representing the U.S.A. and Abilene Christian College in the 1956 Olympics? His haul: gold medals in the 100-meter dash, the 200-meter dash, and the

All-American Sheryl Swoopes addresses forty thousand fans in Jones Stadium, 1993, after the Lady Raiders returned home with the NCAA women's basketball title.

West Texas high school football, early 1900s

400-meter relay. Or TCU's Bob Lilly, Throck-morton's favorite son, who anchored the Dallas Cowboys' Doomsday Defense? Or Texas Tech's man mountain, E. J. Holub, the stalwart of Kansas City's historic Super Bowl victory?

They called Donny Anderson the "Golden Palomino" when he galloped out of tiny Stinnett to shatter rushing records at Texas Tech and break Texans' hearts on New Year's Eve 1967. That's when Anderson spearheaded the final Green Bay drive that lifted Vince Lombardi's Packers to a 21-17 victory over the Dallas Cowboys in the infamous "Ice Bowl." "You grew up today," Lombardi told Anderson with a hug.

Tommy Miller was an off-again, on-again ministerial student and a rookie sports writer when he covered Archer City's victory over the visiting Munday Moguls in a 1960s high school football playoff game. The folks in Archer City shut down the little wooden press box and headed downtown to celebrate. With no place to write, Miller hauled his Under-wood upright typewriter to the Dairy Queen, where many of the fans gathered.

Listening to Miller dictate to the *Abilene Reporter-News* sports desk on the phone, the crowd cheered lustily at each individual high-light of Archer City's first-ever district title. Hearing the ruckus, Miller's editor suspected the young reporter had abandoned Archer City, which was dry, for a beer haul across the Red River. "Where are you, Oklahoma?" the editor yelled into the phone.

In the 1950s in Stamford, the hottest spot in town was Nat Wash's cafe. That was be-cause Gordon Wood's teams were winning and the coach, crowned "the king of the cof-fee shop," held court there every Saturday morning. It didn't hurt business that Nat's three sons—Wayne, Mike, and Joe—were star players.

90

The 1980s brought education reform to Texas, including a proposal to limit football and other extracurricular activities to eight hours weekly. "West Texas was not taken into consideration," grumbled Ballinger School Superintendent Doug Cox. Many roundtrip bus rides on Friday nights would use up the eight-hour quota without so much as playing a down.

In the '90s, the Lenorah Wildcats had another problem—only seven players for their six-man team. Officials canceled football for lack of participation. Then three more boys, though athletically inexperienced, showed up to save the season. Lenorah's story went statewide, headlined "Return of the Wildcats."

In Rotan, they simply called William Henry Govan "H." He was there when Rotan played its first football game, a 6-0 thriller, beating Aspermont in 1923. He was also there sixty years later when they honored him with a larger-than-life granite statue at the Rotan Yellowhammers' game against Hamlin's Pied Pipers.

The team's original waterboy-trainer, Govan performed other duties through the years, including assistant coaching during World War II. "I've seen many a boy come and go," said Govan at his tribute, "and I never did see a bad one." Govan arrived in Rotan by train in 1919, hoping to make six dollars a day at an oil mill. When the mill work played out, he shined shoes at a barber

Willie Govan, the man they called "H," in Rotan, 1973

shop, spent many years as janitor, and eventually acquired his own farm.

His entry into an opposing stadium "almost caused a riot," recalled a Rotan player, because the fans objected to an African-American being part of the team's delegation. Rotan refused to play until officials decided Govan could join the team on the bench. Govan himself never forgot when the Yellowhammers entered a restaurant in a nearby town after another game. "The nigger can't eat in here," the owner said. "What did you say?" Rotan's coach demanded. The owner repeated his statement. "Then there ain't none of us eating in here," said the coach, who loaded the Yellowhammers back on the bus for dinner in Rotan.

"He means a lot to a lot of people and a lot of different things to a lot of different people," said clothier Bill Day. "My two sons played football under him and, in fact, I also played football under him."

Then there was Leonard Buffe, a leathery sheep rancher who doubled as coach of the six-man team in Mullin, population 214. His starting lineup in 1995 was divided between foster children and local talent, subject to his unique discipline. After two players skipped a workout to go fishing, he allowed them to suit up for the next practice. Their assignment: sit on the bench and hold their fishing poles.

Buffe's Bulldogs took on an equally successful team from Colorado, Weldon Valley, in a game ballyhooed as the Super Bowl of Six-Man. A sellout crowd of seventy-eight hundred in Brownwood watched Mullin lose a 58-44 thriller. They came from small towns like Blanket, Strawn, Zephyr, and Gordon. In the stands was an ex-Wichita Falls Coyote, Jan Reid of *Texas Monthly* magazine, whose book *Vain Glory* immortalized Coach Joe Golding's Coyote teams of 1949-61. Of the six-man Super Bowl, Reid wrote, "The game was more than a showcase for football. It was a showcase of pride in their way of life."

Double Mountain Ranch, 1997—Outside, a fierce September sun beat down on the spread Sammy Baugh carved out of rugged flatlands a half century before. The 7,667-acre ranch was named after two peaks that rise unexpectedly out of stringy mesquite, scrub brush, red dirt, and dry creek beds that decorate this lonely part of West Texas.

Frowning slightly, he swore, spit, and leaned back in his chair. His deep blue eyes radiated from a leathery face like twin gemstones embedded in an old and well-worn saddle. "I remember," he said, "when every boy in Texas wanted to go to a Southwest Conference school. They wouldn't even think of going anywhere else." And so it was with him. A high school passing wizard at Sweetwater, he chose football at Texas Christian over a baseball scholarship at Texas. He waited tables and cleaned a campus music room to survive. "I was one of the lucky ones," he said. "I bet there weren't four kids from Sweetwater that went to college. You really appreciated college in those days."

Legendary TCU Coach Dutch Meyer called Baugh the "greatest athlete I ever saw" and, in return, Baugh said, "All the football I knew, I learned from Dutch." Small wonder Baugh, with a whiplike arm, became football's first great passer. He also proved the immortal Grantland Rice wrong when the sportswriter predicted, "He just isn't big enough to take the pounding he's going to get. I doubt a skinny kid like that can last more than a season or two." Baugh spent sixteen years with the Washington Redskins, winning five Eastern Conference titles and two world championships. His versatility was astounding by modern NFL standards. In one pro game, he passed for four touchdowns, and, as a defensive safety, intercepted four passes. One year, he led the NFL in passing, punting, and interceptions.

He directed TCU to twenty-nine victories, including Sugar Bowl and Cotton Bowl

Slingin' Sammy Baugh on his ranch, 1995

championships. But he blamed himself for TCU's loss to SMU before forty thousand fans in Fort Worth for college football's mythical national championship game in 1935. "I've always felt bad about that," Baugh told a reporter many years later. He also was disgruntled about the demise of the Southwest Conference. "Mostly," he said, "they brought it on themselves."

He was self-deprecating about his storied past, grumbling that "there are a lot of old football heroes." He no longer could rope calves, his favorite post-football past time, because of bad knees. "But I'm just as happy as I can be," he said, zinging another shot of Trophy chewing tobacco into a cup. "I wouldn't change a thing in my life."

West Texas, to me, is a little paradise. You have fresh air, the most wonderful weather I have ever experienced in my life—if you overlook the occasional tornado.

15

A West Texan quoted in a collection of oral histories

Strange things happen in West Texas. Foremost, perhaps, is the weather: droughts, floods, tornadoes, dust storms, hail storms, searing heat, and blue northers. Blackie Sherrod, the Dallas sports scribe, says there once was a West Texas county so dry "rainwater was wet only on one side." The Trans-Pecos purportedly was so dry that trees chased dogs. The wind once blew so hard in West Texas that it knocked Roy Rogers off his horse on the drive-in movie screen.

Exaggerations all. But it's a fact that West Texans shielded their dinner tables during the Dust Bowl days by eating under white sheets. There also was a tumbleweed blizzard in Hereford, created by an unsuspecting farmer cutting the thistles from his dormant field. Blown by the winds, they piled up to the rooftops when they hit town.

Years ago, someone staged a rock concert outside Lubbock. It attracted as many state troopers and reporters as paying customers and was memorable only because the hot weather was followed by blowing dirt, rain, cold, and finally an ice storm, all within hours.

The region's number one cash crop, cotton, invariably suffers from too much or too little rain. And when everything is just about

right, hail, boll weevils, or other pests cripple the crops. "It's kind of a mixed bag," sighed one cotton official.

And how's this headline for a mixed bag? "Beneficial Rains Kill 10 People in West Texas."

Once, Governor Dolph Briscoe requested drought relief for West Texas. The next day, the front page of the *Midland Reporter-Telegram* said: "Rains Bring Flood to Odessa . . . Heaviest Rain of the Year."

On June 1, 1998, decades-old high-temperature records fell in Lubbock, where it was 105; Amarillo, 103; Midland, 106; and San Angelo, 105. Temperatures soared to 109 in Wichita Falls and 110 in Childress. By July, a relentless heat wave rivaled the nightmarish summer of 1980 and the drought was killing people, fish, wildlife, vegetation, and cash crops. September brought only scant relief; Fort Worth topped out at 108 degrees. President Clinton made it official: West Texas, along with the rest of the state, was a disaster.

Beating the heat in 1980 was no sweat for builder Jay Swayze of Hereford. He went subterranean with his new home, complete with a swimming pool. "We've gone to the moon and back, and cured a number of common and uncommon ills," he said. "The one thing

A boat dock on Lake J. B. Thomas near Ira rests on the lake bed after the lake lost 95 percent of its capacity in a drought, 1996.

we haven't done is utilize the underground potential."

A freak hail storm near Dalhart once dumped pellets waist-deep, closing farm roads.

On May 11, 1953, a storm system developed over San Angelo, spawning a tornado. It zigzagged in, out, and around several West Texas hamlets as it proceeded eastward. It then ripped the heart out of Waco, killing 114 and injuring 597.

Lethal tornadoes in Lubbock and Wichita Falls and even Hale Center rank among the most destructive in West Texas, but there really was nothing like what occurred at Saragosa on May 22, 1987. The twister descended on the tiny farming center between Fort Davis and Pecos and crushed a

West Texas funnel cloud near Slaton, 1968

Tumbleweeds near Colorado City, circa 1950.

community center where residents were attending a preschool graduation. Thirty people died and more than a hundred were injured. Devastation was everywhere. It was as if a giant sledgehammer slammed the cars and trucks. Trees were debarked or uprooted. The community center and Our Lady of Guadalupe Catholic Church were reduced to strewn piles of debris. "I started to remove some of the walls that collapsed," Herman Tarin said ten years later, recalling how he worked with a backhoe to free victims trapped in the wreckage. "Every time you tried to pick up a piece of the wall, somebody would scream."

They called it Operation Teacup. It was a daily ritual in 1971 at a colorless airport hangar on the outskirts of San Angelo. Scientists and pilots hovered over telephones, fiddled with computers, studied maps, and scowled at the skies. The goal: release silver iodide in the right kind of clouds, hopefully creating rain. "There is no question about the fact that weather patterns have gotten wetter since Teacup was organized," the project manager noted. But "in all honesty," he said, Teacup couldn't claim credit for all the precipitation that occurred.

The lack of rain spawned scores of other attempts to seed West Texas clouds, as well as a minor industry in drought humor and a novel by West Texan Elmer Kelton, *The Time It Never Rained.* There once was a water-witching convention in Quanah, and a more elaborate but unsuccessful attempt to siphon water from suspicious East Texans. The water witches actually found water, but Quanah really caught the national eye when a long-shot rain dance was followed by a rare spring rain.

It hadn't rained appreciably in Midland for eighteen months when Edward Powers began blasting away at the skies in 1891. In his book, *War and Weather,* he asserted that rain followed warfare. The federal government bought his theory to the tune of twelve thousand dollars. Four wagons hauled scientists, crews, and military supplies to the area. The equipment was hardly in place before rain poured for two hours. Unfortunately, the scientists soon learned the downpour was a part of a much larger system throughout the region.

Undeterred, they arranged cannons in a semicircle and fired them in unison at what appeared to be a wisp of a cloud. They planted explosives in prairie dog holes to rattle the ground. They launched ten-foot balloons of oxygen and hydrogen for sky-high explosions. They attached explosives to kites and detonated them electronically. On the experiment's final day, one last balloon was released. About a mile up, it burst. That

evening, heavy clouds formed and workers hurriedly assembled another "electric kite." The blast was followed by a few sprinkles. After more explosions, there was more rain, but it ended altogether the next morning.

In 1902, another rainmaker constructed three tall towers on the North Concho River, pumped clouds of colored gas into the air and sent up balloons loaded with dynamite. History records that some rain fell, but it doesn't say why.

Cereal king C. W. Post adopted the *War and Weather* theory in 1911 and spent three years and a princely fortune simulating military battles along the Caprock. It didn't work.

The folks in Big Spring appealed to a higher power in early 1999. "We rely on the rain here and we rely on God for that rain," said Mayor Tim Blackhear at the opening of the West Texas Rain Rally at the First Baptist Church. As chronicled by the *Big Spring Herald,* the ecumenical gathering drew 750 persons. John Walker, the paper's managing editor, read a letter from the local state senator. Ask God for help, the senator said, because the legislature was helpless to solve the problem. Eddie Tubbs, pastor of the First Baptist Church, called for repentance and read from

Panhandle dust storm, April 14, 1935

Second Chronicles: "If I shut up the heaven that there be no rain . . . If my people, which are called by my name, shall humble themselves and pray and seek my face and turn from the wicked ways, then I will hear from heaven and will forgive their sin and will heal their land."

If nothing else, that should fill up West Texas churches on Sunday.

*T*he state's past drips with drought humor. A century-old example is that of the "droughted-out" farmer who's battling the harsh West Texas climate. Observing that the wagon is pulled by a scrawny mare and ox, a neighbor asks, "Where's your other horse?"

The farmer says, "The drought got so bad old Dollar just up and died on me. So I traded a feller two sections of land for this here ox."

"Steep trade," says the neighbor.

"Well, I offered him one section," says the farmer. "But when we sat down to make out the papers, I found out the damned fool couldn't read, so I stuck him with both sections."

Kent Biffle in "Kent Biffle's Texana," *The Dallas Morning News,* July 14, 1991, quoting from a compilation of drought humor by Rana Williamson

*I*t was a cruel trick, a murderous freak. It formed on a Monday evening in a green sky that offered ominous clues, but descended without warning. "Mother Nature didn't say, 'Hey, here I come,'" a U.S. Weather Bureau official would point out later. The date was May 11, 1970, and it would forever be known as the "Lubbock Tornado." It was an

100

Snow in Palo Duro Canyon

A West Texan's plea, Idalou, 1998

Farmer holds a stalk of cotton near Wilson, 1996. His plants were first burned by drought, then broken by hail, rain, and a sandstorm that followed.

extended nightmare, killing twenty-six, injuring more than five hundred, causing $135 million in damages, leaving thousands homeless and crippling the South Plains city of then 170,000. It was one of the most unusual twisters ever, and also one of the most powerful. Its chaotic path covered fifteen square miles, about a fourth of the city. Several official inspectors said the landscape had the appearance of cities bombed into destruction during wars.

"Rather than moving in on us," said meteorologist Harold Frost, "it developed over us. It would appear it was one giant tornado with strong winds along the sides . . . It was so terribly wide. There are numerous ideas that there were one, two, even three. I can't say I've ever heard nor read of a twister nearly this wide . . . I don't know of anybody who has." Damage indicated the tornado was a mile in breadth and stayed on the ground eight minutes before lifting.

Weather forecasters had reported a radar sighting of a hook, indicating the possible presence of a tornado, in a slow but massive buildup south-southeast of the city. But the biggest factor in the surprise strike resulted from an unusual shift of storm clouds to the northwest—over the center of town—before the twister plunged down.

The weather bureau in Lubbock did issue warnings about the south-southeast hook, but explained that when a tornado funnel develops directly above a city, "there is absolutely no time to get an early warning out." Five years earlier, a vicious storm struck after dark in nearby Hale Center, leaving five dead and forty injured, but civil defense warnings alerted residents of the approaching tornado and saved many lives. "Except for the civil defense warnings . . . it would have just killed people every which way," said Tom Rambo, publisher of the weekly *Hale Center American.*

The Lubbock twister curled down from above the Texas Tech University campus, sparing student dormitories but little else as it spun northeasterly on a collision course with the downtown area, crumbling apartment houses and other dwellings en route. "They said it lasted three to five minutes, but it was an eternity, I'll tell you that," said Ruby Tatum, who was at home with her sister when the storm struck. "I don't know if I was just scared or numb. My two children had just left the house. I thought maybe they were dead somewhere." They weren't, but others were.

The tornado drew a bead on heavily commercial Fourth Street, shredding nearly everything in its path as it pounded into the downtown area. It crippled the city's tallest structure, the twenty-story Great Plains Life Building, which became a lingering peril. Fearing the building would collapse, civil defense officials roamed the streets warning those in the vicinity to "mount up and move out." It was a surrealistic scene. Sound truck amplifiers boomed: "The building is falling! The building is falling!" It never did, but its fate remained in doubt for months.

Approaching Fourth Street, the twister turned into a killer. Leaving the commercial district in a shambles, the tornado veered toward the Guadalupe area, a low income, mostly Hispanic neighborhood. Many of the victims were Hispanic. "All we can do is tag the bodies, fingerprint them, give them a number, and shoot a picture," reported an officer at a junior high school that was converted into a morgue.

Chewing up and spitting out warehouses, utility poles, and buildings, the tornado swept toward residences near the fashionable Lubbock Country Club. Roaring into the Mesa Road area, the storm claimed a family of four. "We didn't know them, but they lived right over there," said a neighbor, pointing at an empty stretch of ground. Leveling expensive homes and slinging their remains onto the fairways and greens of the country club, the storm rumbled on. "We could hear it coming, yet it happened so quick," said Mrs. Larry Duncan. "It was a horrible feeling. First rain, then hail, and then it became very still. And then . . . Boom! Just a boom. And it fell in on us." Mrs. Duncan and her houseguests escaped serious harm, but her husband was hospitalized in shock.

Storm near Canadian

Massive tornado strikes Wichita Falls, 1979

On the storm sped, swooping down at the West Texas Air Terminal to pluck more than a hundred private airplanes from their moorings and scattering them like a flock of dead birds.

In an ironic postscript, it paused to knock out the U.S. Weather Bureau. Then it was gone.

As homeless residents waded through the flooded, littered streets, the black night enveloped the powerless city, illuminated only by the eerie sparks from shorted electrical wires. Dawn brought a dreadful reality, revealing, for the first time, the path the twister had carved into the city. President Nixon declared it a disaster area almost at once. "I don't think anyone could visualize this until he's seen it," said U.S. Senator John Tower, a Republican from Wichita Falls.

As luck—bad luck—would have it, an even more deadly and destructive tornado would slice through Tower's hometown before the decade was out.

A journalist dispatched to Wichita Falls in the early morning hours of April 11, 1979, was stunned not by what he saw but what he couldn't see. There was nothing except darkness. It was pitch black in the downtown area of a city of nearly a hundred thousand. The Wichita Falls Tornado, as the killer storm would be known, had snuffed out both power and water. The streets seemed deserted, perhaps abandoned. It was a little scary, but mostly eerie.

Daybreak revealed the twister had spared the heart of Wichita Falls while carving up the populous suburbs, killing more than forty, injuring more than seventeen hundred, and destroying more than three thousand homes. Damage estimates approached four hundred million dollars.

The incredible but familiar handiwork of one of Texas's most deadly tornadoes was everywhere: leveled homes, shops, and buildings and mangled trees, cars, and utility poles. There was pain, suffering, and heartbreak, scattered looting and price gouging, and the often self-serving and showy arrival of properly grim and grieving political leaders.

One courageous couple mounted a little American flag in the rubble of their home; a For Sale sign rose above another pile of debris that once sheltered a young family. A year later, city planners announced that eighty percent of the destroyed or damaged homes had been rebuilt. Even so, crisis counselors would call it "a very hard year."

The same reporter who saw firsthand the devastation of the 1979 tornado was assigned in 1980 to do an anniversary story. He arrived as a noontime thunderstorm hit, bringing rain, hail, and the trademark turbulence of a killer tornado. "We were almost looking at the same situation as last April 10," meteorologist Frank Cannon would reveal later. The National Weather Service confirmed at least a dozen funnels. Spotters reported a tornado on the ground at Lake Kickapoo in neighboring Archer County. A second funnel touched down just southwest of Wichita Falls, rumbling toward the city. At 12:56 p.m., officials triggered the ominous disaster warning sirens.

At first, the reporter couldn't believe he had come to reexamine the historic 1979 tornado and might have the misfortune of dying in a second one. But he soon came to believe it. Around town, people scurried for cover. They fled from diners, shopping centers, beauty parlors, grocery stores, and elsewhere. Some panicked. Others abandoned their cars—a lesson learned from "Terrible Tuesday" a year earlier. Many took refuge in storm cellars, bathtubs, closets and, in one tragic instance, a drainage ditch. A flash flood drowned a woman and her infant grandchild lying there.

The storm churned through town without further mishap. Even so, the anniversary scare was a unique experience for veterans of the 1979 disaster. Patsy Carroll, her husband, and three children dragged mattresses and pillows into the bathroom, emerging safe but angry. "Something is inherently wrong that we keep fighting the environment," said Mrs. Carroll, whose home was flattened the year before. "I don't like it that we have monster ice storms and monster thunderstorms and monster tornadoes. I can't live the rest of my life running. But I'm mad as hell. I don't like it when I have to listen to my children having nightmares and crying in the night."

Louise Thomas rode out the storm in a cellar with thirteen people and two dogs. As she emerged from the storm cellar, she was relieved to find her newly planted trees still standing. But she, too, was miffed. "I think it's the nerves," she sighed. "It's not so much that I really worry about dying. It's the horror of it all. When we came up last year it was so eerie. That impression will last a lifetime."

I'll be in Hell before you start breakfast, boys, let 'er rip!

16

Texas bandit to his hanging party, as quoted in *Texas Celebrates* by David Kaplan, 1985

West Texan justice often is iffy, perhaps because they don't hang horse thieves any more.

For example, brutality was rivaled only by stupidity when several of Borger's police force chased a fugitive onto the famous Four Sixes Ranch. In the darkness and confusion, the ranch foreman was gunned down in addition to the fugitive. The rancher was hand-cuffed and jerked around before he died.

Enter Racehorse Haynes, the Houston attorney who convinced an Amarillo jury to acquit Fort Worth millionaire Cullen Davis. His legal assault in the Four Sixes case cost the city of Borger a bundle.

Billy Sol did time in La Tuna federal prison, an isolated relic near El Paso, where Mafia informer Joseph Valachi—old, sick, and lonely—spent his last days in maximum security.

David Harris, better known as the husband of folk singer Joan Baez, was also confined at La Tuna, nicknamed The Hacienda. Sentenced for selective service violations, Harris scorned prison authority but caused no major concern.

They sent Liz Chagra of El Paso to the federal pen in Fort Worth. Her crime:

delivering $250,000 from her husband to pay off assassin Charles Harrelson in the murder of federal Judge John Wood Jr. Ms. Chagra, forty-three, contracted ovarian cancer and then spent more than three years petitioning authorities for her freedom. "I try not to take this personally," she told *The Dallas Morning News*. "I think the Prison Board is trying to tell me, 'OK, Liz, you are going to die in prison and that's it.'" She was right.

Former U.S. Housing Secretary Henry Cisneros had legal problems that stretched from Washington, D.C. to Lubbock. In Lubbock, his former mistress pleaded guilty to twenty-eight counts of conspiracy, bank fraud, money laundering, and obstruction of justice. Said she at sentencing: "I did not know it was a crime. I take full responsibility for it, but I did not know it was a crime."

The "Mum Lady," Mary Gunnels of Brownfield, had reason to plead ignorance. She was nabbed by authorities for making and selling homecoming mums from her home. She fought the charges and won. She ran for mayor and lost.

In the rolling, brittle woodlands west of LBJ Country, they called the Parkers "Big Ranch, Old West." The Parker clan was

State trooper at a roadblock during Republic of Texas siege near Fort Davis, 1997

linked by blood to both the Alamo and Comanche Chief Quanah Parker. James Henry Parker hauled rocks from the Little Devil's River to build a home in the early 1870s for his bride Tildy, a grandniece of Davy Crockett. The couple's original 160-acre tract would grow to twelve thousand acres—called Old Ranch by the family. So began the story of scarlet bloodlines, so twisted and tragic that it reached across four generations.

Jim and Tildy Parker produced eleven children, one of whom, Jess, moved to Old Ranch in the 1930s and ran cattle until his death at the age of ninety-seven. Called "Big Daddy," Jess set aside separate parcels for his offspring, but relations between two of the brothers weren't as harmonious as he would have wished. Cancer took one brother in 1968, and his widow and children were reluctantly urged to leave by Big Daddy "before something bad happens." The banishment was undone in 1986 when Big Daddy died and his will restored the land to the family in exile. Grandson Bruce Parker jumped at the chance to return.

Within two years, three Parkers, including Bruce, would be dead, all from gunshot wounds. One, a nephew of Big Daddy, perished in an apparent robbery attempt, although a relative wasn't so sure of the circumstances. Bruce was next. His body was found sprawled in the dirt on the driver's side of his pickup near a favorite river overlook. His .22-caliber rifle and his Ruger pistol were on the passenger seat. Authorities initially ruled his death was suicide, but Bruce's skeptical wife Linda persuaded a Texas Ranger to investigate further.

The shock came on November 17 with the indictment of Doyle Parker, the brother who stayed on Old Ranch when Bruce and his mother were banished. A Kimble County grand jury said he "intentionally and knowingly" killed Bruce. Among those providing secret testimony was Doyle's brother Raymond, who maintained ties with Bruce during his exile. Less than a month later,

Raymond picked up his .22-caliber automatic pistol and disappeared into the bathroom of his ranch home. Without a word, or even a note, he blew his brains out.

The legal drama eventually moved to San Angelo on a change of venue after the defense argued that Doyle Parker was incompetent to stand trial for Bruce's death because of his advanced age. District Attorney Ron Sutton scoffed: "His mother's in good shape at ninety-two and his father lived to be ninety-seven. These people live forever down there unless they get shot." It was almost anticlimactic that Doyle Parker was found guilty by a San Angelo jury. As one investigator explained, "The family got larger and larger and the land smaller and smaller."

Rancher J. Frank Norfleet described himself as "one of the biggest suckers of all time." And he became nationally famous because of it. Norfleet was on business in Dallas in 1919 when a couple of strangers persuaded him to put thirty thousand dollars into a cotton speculation deal. Then they disappeared. For five years, Norfleet checked hotel registers, pursued countless tips, and traveled more than forty thousand miles across the United States and Canada. As a result, arrests were made in San Bernardino, California, Oklahoma City, Jacksonville, Florida, and Salt Lake City. He wrote a book, *Norfleet,* and earned a national reputation for tracking other swindlers. But he always returned to his ranch near Hale Center, which he bought in 1907 while working as a cowboy for a dollar a day.

The Norfleets' door "was always open to those in need," said his obituary in 1967, "and during the days of the wagon trains, fifty-four people reportedly stayed at the home at one time." He died at the age of 102, but not before he offered this formula for a long life: "I don't drink, chew tobacco, smoke, cuss or tell lies. The last is the most important though—I never tell a damn lie."

For thirteen years, investigators in Wichita Falls thought they were searching for three different murderers in the deaths of Terry Lee Sims, Toni Gibbs, and Ellen Blau. The three young women had been raped, stabbed, and suffocated during an eighteen-month period. But the official theory changed in the spring of 1999 when new DNA technology led authorities back to a familiar face, Farylon Edward Wardrip. Wardrip was a parolee living and even teaching Sunday School in Olney after serving eleven years of a thirty-five-year sentence for the 1986 murder of still another young woman from Wichita Falls. This time around, officers charged him with murder in the death of Ms. Sims and tossed him back in jail while questioning him about the other slayings as well. "It feels good to know that someone was still looking into this case," said Catherine Reid, Ms. Sims's sister. "My sister deserves justice, even though it's been a long time coming."

Justice was delayed—but not denied—in the bizarre case of Ralph Erdmann, who was West Texas's main forensic pathologist in the 1980s, handling bodies for forty-eight counties. Among his more gruesome errors were a misplaced head and parts from two different corpses packed in the same container. Erdmann once ruled a woman's death was accidental, but it was determined later she had been smothered by her former lover.

Then there was the "Friday the 13th Murder," the stuff of horror stories. On that July night in 1990, seventeen-year-old Frankie Garcia of Panhandle was lured to a dilapidated barn near a deserted shack known as the Haunted House. The killer forced him to his knees, stuck a rifle barrel in his mouth and pulled the trigger. The gunman was Kenneth Glenn Milner, nineteen, a handsome, self-styled satanist. Friends said Milner was obsessed with death, horror movies, and creating special effects like those used in slasher movies. After Milner pled guilty, Judge John Forbis declared, "What you have done is the most heinous, heartless event that has ever occurred in the history of the 100th Judicial District."

We assumed the authorities would do their job. 17

Norbert Schlegel, after learning of his daughter's death

A neighbor recalled hearing an unusual sound on a fateful spring day in Rotan. A sound she interpreted as a cry of distress. "A human sound," she said. When she entered the nearby brick home of Rhonda and Bobby Templin, she found twenty-year-old Rhonda lying on the floor, her nude and lifeless body covered by a blanket. Rhonda's husband Bobby appeared overcome with grief and close to hysteria. He was crying and pacing the floor and banging his head against the wall. Bobby said Rhonda was bathing when a radio fell into the tub, electrocuting her. He lifted her body from the tub and carried it to the living room. He then telephoned for help.

The death of blond, blue-eyed Rhonda Templin in 1976 stunned and saddened the residents of Rotan, a windblown hamlet deep in the heart of West Texas. She was simply too young, too pretty, and too loving to die so suddenly and so harshly. And so carelessly.

By nightfall, a justice of the peace ruled the death accidental. But the story of Rhonda and Bobby Templin did not end on that tragic Sunday. Some could even argue that the story might never run its tangled and twisted course. Even so, almost everyone came to believe Bobby killed his high school sweetheart in cold blood and covered up the crime so cleverly that small-town authorities suspected nothing for months, even years. The disclosure was due largely to a relentless and costly inquiry by Rhonda's grieving parents,

who finally aroused the suspicions of skeptical authorities. Norbert and Jaye Nell Schlegel eventually uncovered circumstantial but compelling evidence that their daughter's death was not an accident.

A few insisted it was not the scattered clues and revelations that brought about Bobby's downfall. It was his freewheeling, extramarital sex life that upset folks in the small West Texas town. "Bobby was a womanizer," his attorney conceded, "and everybody in town knew it . . . If this case had been tried in Dallas or Houston they'd never have convicted him."

Bobby Templin and Rhonda Schlegel grew up in the pleasant community of Shamrock in the Texas Panhandle, 180 miles north of Rotan. Rhonda was a bouncy, bright-eyed cheerleader with platinum blond hair, a quick smile, and a crush on maybe the best-looking kid at Shamrock High School. She was the second of four children of Norbert and Jaye Nell Schlegel, a hardworking, middle-class couple who themselves grew up in Shamrock, were high school sweethearts, and married in 1952.

When the Schegels learned of their daughter's death, they left at once for Rotan. Upon arrival, they confronted Bobby, demanding to know what happened. Unaccountably, Bobby seemed unwilling or unable to tell them. Norbert immediately sensed something amiss, terribly so. But years would pass before his darkest suspicions could be confirmed.

A neighbor and nursing supervisor named Alta Hinson had been among the first to respond to a call from Bobby for help. Entering the bathroom, Mrs. Hinson saw a radio submerged in the tub along with part of an extension cord and a towel. Later, with police permission, she removed the radio from the tub and noticed the wires on the extension cord were exposed near one end. They had been severed and spliced back together. She wrapped the cord around the radio and placed it in a cabinet beneath the vanity, where Jaye Nell found it while searching for an aspirin. She summoned Norbert. "I know Rhonda wouldn't have used that," her husband said when shown the exposed wires. "She knew better."

On the long drive back to Shamrock that Sunday night, Norbert wondered how the cord got mangled and why, when spliced back, the wires were not taped or somehow insulated. He wondered about the radio, where it had come from, and when. He had not seen it on previous visits. And why would Rhonda choose a cheap radio over her new stereo if she wanted music while she bathed?

That raised still another question. The Schlegels knew their daughter showered daily but never bathed. And something else: Bobby left the house to buy gas when the accident purportedly occurred. But his car was less than half full when he accompanied the Schlegels to Shamrock.

After the funeral, Jaye Nell and her sister discovered another curious item: a new extension cord lying in plain sight in a kitchen cabinet. The implications were obvious: Why would Rhonda use a damaged and dangerous cord with a new one at her fingertips? But even as Jaye Nell came to share her husband's suspicions about Bobby, the couple was confident that authorities would investigate their daughter's death and act on the evidence they were uncovering.

"We learned it was not that simple," Norbert recalled with a humorless smile. Actually, the Schlegels' attempt to persuade authorities to investigate Rhonda's death was cursed from the start. There was no obvious evidence to suggest homicide. Incredibly, not a single investigative agency examined the autopsy photographs until months later, and then only at the insistence of the Schlegels.

But even Norbett and Jaye Nell overlooked the implications of burns on the inside of Rhonda's right arm and the adjacent side of her right breast. And, hindsight suggests also that someone would have come forward to reveal Bobby's philandering. But no one did so at once. It was almost as if there was a benign conspiracy of silence.

With no alternative, the Schlegels began asking their own questions, traveling constantly from Shamrock to Rotan, Roby, Sweetwater, Snyder, Abilene, Colorado City, and elsewhere around that area of West Texas. Although Bobby was not oblivious to what was going on, the Schlegels maintained a friendly facade, and he probably underestimated their resolve. He also "told us things that we knew were not true," said Jaye Nell.

The Schlegels eventually discovered Bobby and their daughter had taken out an accidental death policy through a bank club even though Bobby originally said there was no insurance. He had collected ten thousand dollars in June and used it to pay bills.

A sales clerk named Wanda Kiker told a friend of Rhonda's that she sold a radio to someone matching Bobby's age and description in nearby Roby just days before their daughter's death. The Schlegels would also learn that the customer removed the backs and examined the cords of two small radios before paying thirty-five dollars cash for one of them. By then, however, the radio taken from the bathtub had vanished.

Norbert and Jaye Nell hounded the district attorney's office with such fervor that they finally attracted the attention of a sharp

Rhonda Templin of Rotan

young assistant district attorney named Rusty Carroll and a D.A.'s investigator named Kenneth Crow. Crow was present when the Schlegels arranged a visit with the Abilene pathologist who performed the autopsy on Rhonda's body. It was a pivotal trip. Crow spotted the "mirror image" burns under Rhonda's right arm. "It was the bare wire under the arm where the juice entered the body," Crow said later. "When I saw that, there was no way I could figure out how this was an accident." As unyielding as a mesquite, Crow was something of a legend in his part of Texas, and suddenly the Schlegels had a critical ally. "Keep looking, keep investigating, and keep telling me things," Crow advised the Schlegels. He also told them to look beyond the reign of his current boss to the day when Rusty Carroll took over as district attorney. "When Rusty becomes D.A., this could become a prosecutable case," he said.

Sure enough, in January 1981, nearly five years after Rhonda's death, District Attorney Frank Ginzel retired and Rusty Carroll succeeded him. Unlike his predecessor, the spunky young Carroll was not burdened with doubts about Bobby's guilt or qualms about prosecuting him. Also, the tireless Schlegels had found an unlikely expert witness for their case. Acting on a tip, they gathered up autopsy reports, photographs, and anything else they could lay their hands on and drove three hundred miles to Dallas to see Dr. Vincent DiMaio, chief pathologist at the Dallas Institute of Forensic Science.

Later, Norbert recalled the meeting this way: "DiMaio looked at everything. He read the autopsy report and looked at the photographs and then called in another doctor, Patrick Besant-Matthews. Dr. Matthews was the foremost expert in electrical deaths and had been in Dallas only two months. He reviewed the information and said, 'This was a homicide. And I'll testify to that.'"

The Schlegels also picked up a startling bit of information from Bobby's relatives. Two of his young cousins claimed Bobby once bragged that he and his older brother Jim had electrocuted dogs and cats while youngsters in Dallas. "He said that they peeled some wires back on an extension cord, and hooked them to the dog or cat, and then plugged them in," one cousin said. "Sometimes it killed them and sometimes it didn't." This wasn't a "smoking gun," but in a classic circumstantial evidence case, it was a loaded and dangerous weapon. It demonstrated Bobby's familiarity with electricity and its use to kill or maim.

On April 21, 1981, five years and ten days after Rhonda's death, a Fisher County grand jury indicted Bobby Templin for murder. Seven months later, the State of Texas launched its case in a Roby courtroom jammed with spectators, many of them openly skeptical of the criminal charges. "Just wait a few days and watch," Rusty Carroll countered with a smile. He then set about proving beyond a reasonable doubt that Bobby placed a "live bare-wire extension cord" to his wife's chest as she lay in the bathtub, fatally shocking her. The prosecution would contend that the current caused Rhonda's arm to contract against the wire, clamping it there and causing the mirror burn images. Being partially submerged in water, she would have been unable to resist or defend herself. Moreover, the electricity would pass through the body into the bathtub water, explaining the absence of exit wounds.

Carroll, armed also with the fruits of the Schlegels' relentless investigation, spent several days laying out the state's circumstantial case. At week's end, Judge Weldon Kirk's courtroom was overflowing with spectators scrambling for prime spots on the front row. It now seemed certain that Bobby's fate hinged on his own appearance before the jury of five women and seven men.

Defense attorney Charlie Scarborough, a tough legal blueblood from Abilene, led Bobby through a series of critical denials aimed at the heart of the state's case. Even so, Bobby was his own worst enemy. During a break, he entertained his giggling female fan club by flashing a sign that read, "I'm the bad guy." After Bobby swore from the witness stand he did not kill Rhonda, it was Rusty Carroll's turn for cross-examination. "Rusty crucified him," Ken Crow would declare years later. "Bobby was a lousy witness."

Jurors apparently agreed. In a case that took five and a half years to bring to trial, and then only because of Rhonda's grieving and relentless parents, the verdict was swift and decisive: Guilty. A short time later, after the punishment phase, the jurors returned with the maximum penalty: ninety-nine years in prison. Norbert and Jaye Nell were speechless.

An appellate court subsequently upheld the conviction, and Bobby remained in prison at Huntsville until April 23, 1986, when the Texas Court of Criminal Appeals ruled that Rusty Carroll went too far in using the "plugging-up-puppies" issue to demonstrate prior misconduct on Bobby's part. Bobby, then thirty-two, was released on bail and remained free for eight months while a new trial was scheduled and a special prosecutor was appointed to try the case. Rusty Carroll had moved on to a new job in Bell County, and the new district attorney could not prosecute because he once represented Bobby.

The special prosecutor, Pete Greene, was impressed with the Schlegels' investigative efforts. "Their persistence and involvement was probably a better approach in the long run," said Greene, a former district attorney. "If a guy with a badge tried to get the same information, he wouldn't have gotten it." This time, it took the new West Texas jury ninety minutes to convict Bobby of murder and just thirty minutes to assess punishment, once again at ninety-nine years in the Texas Department of Corrections.

All Fort Worth natives are cowboys, even those who aren't.

Sheila Taylor Wells, Fort Worth columnist

18

Despite the Abilenes and Muleshoes, the Spurs and the Herefords, there is no place in West Texas that more vividly reflects the image of this vast and versatile region than Fort Worth. Sure, it's known worldwide as "The City Where the West Begins," but what does that mean? For one thing, Fort Worth truly is the gateway to West Texas. The famous Chisholm Trail passed nearby, but also consider this: from Fort Worth, U.S. 287 leads to the Panhandle; U.S. 180 leads to the Caprock; U.S. 377 leads to Brownwood and beyond; Interstate 20 leads to El Paso.

Aside from the Chisholm, few trails anywhere are as famous, or infamous, as old Texas 199, which winds northwest out of Fort Worth to Jacksboro on a line toward Amarillo. Nicknamed "Thunder Road," the Jacksboro Highway once was a microcosm of Fort Worth itself. In the "good old bad days," as one of the veteran players called it, Thunder Road was a gaudy mix of burglars and bootleggers, rogues and royalty, whores and hit men, rednecks and roughnecks, and college kids on the prowl. It was cold beer and hot dice and warm summer nights spent dancing under the stars at Lake Worth. It was murder and mayhem, cops and robbers, rhythm and blues, and the big band sounds of Billy May and Paul Whiteman. It was the Rocket, the Skyliner, the Black Cat, the Showboat, the

Barrel, the Casino, the 3939, the Four Deuces, the Coconut Grove, the Bad Liquor, Club 21, and the lure of a young baby-faced stripper named Candy Barr.

It was simply a ten-mile neon ribbon of revelry, a crude symbol of Fort Worth's rough-and-tumble heritage, and a playground for the brave, bold, adventuresome, and foolhardy. The lights flickered and dimmed years ago and, with the millennium, the party's about over. But the memories linger on, spiced by a bit of myth and more than a dash of truth. Anyone who's been there is an expert. Listen . . .

Robert White: "When they widen that highway, they'll probably find a whole bunch of skeletons."

Cliff Helton: "Liquor laws? Practically nil. Everyone had a bootlegger."

Carolyn Miller: "They weren't all killers. They just loved to fight."

Jess Johnson: "There were more cathouses up and down the Jacksboro Highway than you could shake a stick at."

Cleon Nettles: "When someone got too big for his britches, he just disappeared . . . and they'd find him in a well."

Bobby Eubanks: "The farther you went, the badder it got. You could get into anything you were big enough to handle."

The boom begins. McClesky No. 1 blows in near Ranger, 1917.

Mr. West Texas, the late Amon Carter met with the first Board of Directors, Texas Technological College in Sweetwater, Texas, March 2, 1923. Front row, left to right: C. W. Meadows, Secretary; Silliman Evans (not a Director, Staff Correspondent, Fort Worth Star-Telegram); Ex-Governor W. P. Hobby; Mrs. F. N. Drane; Governor Pat M. Neff. Back, row left to right: R. A. Underwood, Vice Chairman; Clifford B. Jones, Treasurer; Dr. J. E. Nunn; Amon G. Carter, Chairman; J. W. Carpenter. Missing is Mrs. Charles DeGroff.

A customer at Massey's Club 21: "I really liked the old Tower Motel. The popular phrase was, 'Let's go to the Tower for an hour.'"

Byron Matthews: "You ever hear of Elmer Sharp? Nobody ever whipped him. I don't mean he was such a good fighter, he was just tough." A customer at the Scoreboard on the other side of town said, "Elmer Sharp was so tough he wrestled his pet bear. But his mama was tougher."

As a youngster growing up on Thunder Road, Pat Kirkwood scrambled atop the roof of his dad's gambling joint on Saturday nights and assessed the economy by activities along the road below. "If it was a three-ambulance evening, money was a little tight," he recalled. "But seven or eight ambulances meant everything was okay. People were out spending money and boozing and brawling."

It was Kirkwood who called them "the good old bad days." Well, the good old days are gone, and what's left of Thunder will eventually be a new freeway. Critically wounded by urban growth, changing lifestyles, and its own wicked reputation, the highway has become in recent years an eyesore and a toothless lion. But it provided an extraordinary ride for a generation or two of rowdy Texans during a marvelously wild and evil era.

Farewell, Thunder.

In October 1917, a wildcat well gushed in at Ranger, ninety miles west of Fort Worth. The discovery touched off furious drilling activity. Spectacular discovery wells came in at Eastland, Cisco, Breckenridge and numerous other sites west of Fort Worth. A tiny hamlet known to some as Hogtown mushroomed from fifty residents to sixteen thousand within months. Long the regional headquarters for the cattle industry, Fort Worth awoke to find itself the center for far-ranging oil speculation as well.

"Ranger was a muddy boomtown with scarcely a wooden sidewalk, no hotels, and only a few boarding houses and tents to rent," noted author Mack Williams in *Oil Legends of Fort Worth*. "Oilmen from every part of the nation and abroad headed for Fort Worth, instead." They checked into the Westbrook Hotel. Williams's account continued:

The twelve-story Westbrook became the world's oil center . . .

Chairs and couches were cleared from the lobby to provide more room for oilmen making deals, and to prevent them from sleeping there when all rooms were booked. Management decreed that guests could keep a room for only ten days, and charged

sky-high rent even for cots in the hallway.

In the lobby, a statue of a thinly-clad woman dubbed "the Golden Goddess" presided over a frantic scene that parallels today's New York Stock Exchange trading pit . . . West Texans, enriched by oil, moved to Fort Worth and built mansions in Ryan Place, Park Hill and Rivercrest. Skyscrapers rose downtown. Less than a year after the Ranger discovery, Fort Worth ranked seventh among U.S. cities in new construction . . .

Refineries were built. The city became a great pipeline center, a major hub in a national industry that promised to expand each year as automobiles replace the horse.

All this, and hardly a drop of oil has ever been found in and around Fort Worth itself.

We were young buck teenagers, Future Farmers of America in from West Texas, come to the big city, our dreams as big and showy as the yellow school buses we rode in on . . .

This was my first visit to the most important city I had ever heard about: Fort Worth. Wild and wonderful Fort Worth. Panther City, Cowtown, the great city to the east that not just touched but gave sustenance to the soul of all of prairie and pasture. Capital of West Texas, capital of Texas and the world, for all we knew. Home of the Leonard's store and its incomparable Christmas Toyland. Home of Texas Christian University and the all-Americans Jim Swink and Bob Lilly. Home of cattle barons and oil millionaires and the Amon Carter family and the Star-Telegram—My Lord, was there really any reason for another newspaper to exist, my wise old neighbor, Mr. Gilbreath, used to ask.

But mostly, it was home of our heritage, a proud and swaggering city of spirit and verve that affirmed, over and over, the very reasons for walking tall: It was not, so this city-town of the West proclaimed with an evangelical fervor, just a passive pleasure to grow up West Texan. There was nothing better this side of heaven.

Mike Blackman, native of Anson, writing in the *Fort Worth Star-Telegram* in 1994, about a trip to the Fort Worth Stock Show

Despite its storybook history, Fort Worth, like its smaller sister cities to the west, has had its share of downs as well as ups. A reporter writing about Fort Worth was moved to wonder: "Cowtown or Cowchip?" Said one cynic: "A great place to live, but I wouldn't want to visit there." The city's unofficial motto suggests it had a problem with self-esteem: "Fort Worth—Love It or Leave It." A long ago visitor, presumably from Dallas, brushed off Fort Worth with the following slight: "The town was so dull that a panther was found asleep on Main Street." That was the forerunner to the dubious nickname, "Panther City."

Back then, Fort Worth embraced the benevolent legacy of publisher Amon G. Carter, the fundamentalist doctrine of crusading sensationalist J. Frank Norris, and a flip-side tradition of gangland violence. The blue northers that rattled a cowman's teeth later chapped the cheeks of bankers and lawyers as they shuffled through the canyons between downtown skyscrapers. But it was still a town with ultra-bright wino blight and a loutish but amusing political history. A legislative candidate once described his opponent as "such a tool of the loan sharks that he ought to live in an aquarium." To the distress

of the Fort Worth Chamber of Commerce, city fathers once discovered that the chamber's executive director was living in suburban Arlington.

Then, Fort Worth and its checkered image changed dramatically, reaching a flash point in 1998 with the opening of the sixty-five-million-dollar Nancy Lee and Perry R. Bass Performance Hall. The opening of Bass Hall was a milestone in the transformation of Cowtown into "Wowtown." The Carnegie Hall of Cowtown became a monument to the classics just as Billy Bob's mammoth honky-tonk across town was a citadel of country. Native son Joe Nick Patoski, writing in *Texas Monthly*, described Bass Hall as the "crowning achievement of the renaissance of a city center that had been left for dead twenty-five years ago."

A writer from New York, David Langford, was even more impressed:

> The Fort Worth/Tarrant County Convention Center and the spectacular Water Gardens sit on what was once known as "Hell's Half Acre," a raunchy neighborhood of brothels and saloons where cattlemen mingled with gamblers and outlaws, and cowpokes had a final fling before herding their cattle up the Chisholm Trail to Kansas. Butch Cassidy and the Sundance Kid were among the unsavory habitués around 1900 . . .
> Restored to their original Victorian beauty are fourteen blocks of red brick streets and courtyards lined with upscale restaurants and specialty shops, galleries, museums, lounges and nightclubs . . .

Langford also gushed about the Caravan of Dreams, a venue for the nation's top jazz artists; Burnett Park, which features a series of sculptures by French artist Henri Matisse; and *The Chisholm Trail*, a three-story trompe l'œil mural in Sundance Square. He listed

Chisholm Trail mural on building in Fort Worth's revitalized downtown, 1999

Fort Worth's internationally famous Van Cliburn piano competition and world-class museums, the Kimbell and the Carter, but our Yankee writer seemed most impressed by the city's raunchy old stockyards, now a national historic district.

Cowgirls and cowboys dance the Texas Two-Step and swill Lone Star Beer at Billy Bob's Texas, "the world's largest honky-tonk," where the icons of country music often perform . . .

Live country music also can be heard at the old White Elephant Saloon where each Feb. 8 there's a reenactment of the 1887 gunfight between White Elephant's owner Luke Short and "Long Hair Jim" Courtwright, a former marshal.

Our Yankee writer seemed surprised that Luke always wins.

The trees are so low 'round here, rustlers got to be hung laying down.

Unknown Panhandle resident

19

Former Potter County Judge Hugh Russell stared out the window of Amarillo's tallest building and reckoned that it's terribly hard to photograph the Panhandle. "It just keeps on going," he mused. "There's nothing to frame it in."

Some say it's flat. If so, they have never driven among the rugged buttes along Boys Ranch Road or gazed upon the moonscape of the Canadian River breaks outside of Borger.

Some say it's boring. If so, they've never seen the soaring thunderheads of a summer storm, or a pheasant flushed from a bar ditch by a passing car.

Some say it's never ending. If so, they agree with Richard Robinson, who once said, "You can get out here and stretch your eyeballs. I like trees and all that, but I also like to see where I'm going."

The vast open space is, in fact, staggering. Consider the circumstances of Tennessee-born Molly Goodnight in the late 1800s, living alone while husband Charles was driving cattle to market. It was seventy-five miles to the nearest neighbor. The nearest village was two hundred miles away. Her first house, according to historian James L. Haley, was a "mud-chinked cedar pole dugout" at the bottom of the Palo Duro Canyon. Her conversation companions: three chickens that "knew me and tried to talk to me in their own language."

Back then, fewer than two thousand settlers called the Panhandle home. The largest community was Tascosa, the Wild West in every way. "Follow the trail of empty whiskey bottles" were the directions once given Sam Houston's son, Temple, as he began his first journey to the Panhandle's roughest town. Saloons served thirsty cowboys and so did a red-light district named Hogtown. There was even a cemetery called Boot Hill and enough outlaw gunfights for it to earn its name. Creole-born Frenchy McCormick dealt cards in her husband's rowdy casino, where the clientele included Billy the Kid and Bat Masterson.

Tascosa quickly fell victim to changing times. The range wars led to the Panhandle's huge ranches being encircled by barbed wire, cutting off Tascosa's wagon trade. When the Fort Worth and Denver City Railroad arrived in the region, workers stopped at a place called Ragtown—a crude collection of dwellings covered with buffalo hides. Ragtown's now known as Amarillo. The frontier town of Tascosa is no more.

The Texas Panhandle still is defined more by what there isn't than what there is. It isn't close to the Texas capital; in fact, the capitals of *six* other states are nearer to at least one Panhandle town than Austin. Which ones? Santa Fe, New Mexico, of course. And, obviously, Oklahoma City. Topeka, Kansas, even

Amateur cowboy Frank Winters takes his turn at saddle bronc riding, XIT Rodeo, Dalhart.

Denver, Colorado. Also Lincoln, Nebraska—a stretch, but true. The sixth is faraway Cheyenne, in Wyoming, a portion of which the independent nation of Texas once claimed.

There's no ocean for the Panhandle, just wave after wave of grain—sorghum, mostly, to feed the cattle now crowded into feedlots instead of grazing on the open range. There aren't many trees, either. On the other hand, there was a fellow who returned from a business trip, complaining, "They've damn sure got a tree problem back East."

There's no mountain range, but an incredible hole—the Palo Duro Canyon—majestic in its depth. There's no more rousing sight than the riders on the canyon rim, holding the translucent Texas flag against the sunset, as the night summer pageant *TEXAS* begins.

As for entertainment, there's Friday night football, be it the Pampa Harvesters or the Golden Wolves from Dalhart. But there aren't enough Texas opponents to tackle, so teams have traveled to New Mexico, Oklahoma, and even Kansas. No problem filling a schedule for girls' basketball, however. It may be the Panhandle's most enduring sport.

Often, there's no relief from the cold—they call it the Canadian Express—when the thermometer has dipped to twenty below. Or the heat—120 degrees was once recorded. Or the drought, like the one that created the Dust Bowl of the 1930s. Still, there have been optimists like the late Speedy Nieman, Hereford's kindest soul, who once said, "We're one day closer to our next rain."

There's no hot air in a farmhand's speech, even though most of the nation's helium is produced nearby.

No more Comanches, once rulers of the plain. The last great Indian battle was at Adobe Walls, where a relative handful of buffalo hunters held off a raiding party of seven hundred Comanche, Kiowa, and Cheyenne led by Lone Wolf and Quanah Parker.

No buffalo, either. The buffalo hunters took care of that.

Take a long look at the T-square perfect horizon—not empty, but spare and clean, punctuated by the perpendicular of grain elevators in the distance. There are gullies, cedar breaks, lofty cottonwoods, mesas, a riverbed here and there, a playa lake when water has nowhere to go, but mostly there's plain.

Larry McMurtry had it right in *Dead Man's Walk* when young Gus and Call

Panhandle treasure Palo Duro Canyon State Park

trekked across the Panhandle with the ill-fated Santa Fe expedition: "After a day or two on the llano, the meaning of distance seemed changed. The great plain, silent and endless, became the world. In relation to the plain, they felt like ants. The smaller world of towns and creeks and clumps of forest seemed difficult to remember."

To the east above the Red River is Oklahoma, the western portion of which possesses similar character but not the mystique. To the north is the Midwest, without the Panhandle's cowboy past. To the west is New Mexico, emptier still. To the south is the Texas South Plains and Lubbock, but never, never make the mistake of calling that the Panhandle. It offends both territories.

Bank teller, Hereford, early 1900s

A Texan living in Connecticut once portrayed his native land as "a natural high—a place to be loose; skinny-dip in the hollow; make love under the stars, eat enchiladas, barbecue and catfish; and enjoy life on a per diem basis." Throw in a windmill, a pump-jack, a barbecue cafe, a rumpled cowhand, the golden buffalo grass, and the blazing sun, and you've got the Texas Panhandle. As the day fades, the sky is shrimp pink close to the ground, spreading between fingers of purple and into the starlit dome above. At other times, a hailstorm instantly fills the ditches. The spine of a tornado can be observed for miles.

There's much to love *and* loathe. Like the rest of West Texas, it may seem at times that "everything stings, sticks, or stinks," the complaint of an early visitor. But there is a cowboy breakfast many cool mornings on the rim of the Palo Duro, where biscuits are cooked in a cast-iron Dutch oven. There is the Alibates National Monument near Fritch, a mining site that's millennia old.

There's no longer a residential Panhandle community of Phillips, because the giant petroleum company by the same name bought the land underneath the houses. Faced with eviction, the residents sued. The town then literally moved—on rollers—to other locations.

There's still the little burg of Bovina down the road from Hereford, the latter once known as the "Town without A Toothache." Natural fluoride is in the water supply.

Dawn's on one side of the Panhandle, Goodnight on the other.

There's Lark and Quail, and even Turkey, where the Hotel Turkey has never been closed. Said a writer for *Texas Monthly,* "It was so quiet one cloudy morning that my sneeze sounded like a rifle shot." First called Turkey Roost, the town is best known for the annual Bob Wills Reunion, when its population of five hundred swells to more than twenty times that.

James Rob Wills's daddy was a fiddler, so it was natural he became one, too. Theirs was a struggling existence, farming cotton, so Jim Rob—Bob—played on weekends at ranch dances. His biographer, Charles Townsend, said Bob invented his style—a brand new music that could be called Western jazz—from southern breakdown tunes and the blues of African-Americans with whom he worked in the fields. Bob "ah-hah'ed" his way through five decades, last playing as a virtual invalid to an audience in Big Spring in 1973. Later that year, he sat with the Texas Playboy greats, including Leon McAliffe, on the front end of a nostalgic recording session in Dallas.

His wife Betty carried him back to Fort Worth, where he watched TV for a few minutes and then asked her to "roll me down." Those were his last words.

Panhandle people often feel ignored. "I think the Panhandle of Texas ought to secede and form a state of its own," said Betty Biggs, the feisty editor of a weekly newspaper in the town of Panhandle. Her city manager, Larry Gilley, could not fully agree, but he conceded, "When you live this far from Austin, you always have in the back of your mind that they don't know you exist."

A writer once theorized that the Texas Panhandle's population had more in common with the citizens of other panhandles throughout the nation than perhaps their own state. A newspaper poll in Nebraska's Panhandle showed that readers preferred to join neighboring Wyoming instead of remaining Cornhuskers. Lottery, horse racing, and riverboat gambling received strong support from West Virginia's Panhandle, whereas the citizens downstate thought it was the "devil's work." Florida's Panhandle voters wanted to join Alabama in 1870, but the legislature failed to act. In Idaho's Panhandle, the bars are open; such customs offend the south.

Points discovered in the flint quarries at Alibates National Monument near Borger.

Grain elevator, Hereford

Storing the grain, early 1900s

The King of Western Swing, Bob Wills (center: clapping) and his band (Wade Ray, fiddler). The Showboat, Las Vegas, June, 1959

That kind of independence would have appealed to Ben Ezell, who spent forty-five years at the helm of the weekly *Record* in the town of Canadian. Friends and colleagues insisted his honesty and fairness were exceeded only by his courage. He opposed an incompetent county sheriff, John Birchers, and a politician who wanted to bomb North Vietnam into a pile of sand. "I've been here forty-three years, and I've only been worked over once," he told a reporter for the *Amarillo Globe-News* in 1991. The work-over occurred in 1955 when Ezell was on the losing end of a fistfight with a mayoral candidate unhappy

with an editorial. In 1971, someone, presumably another irate *Record* reader, blew nineteen holes in the office door with a pellet gun. "Someone was expressing an editorial opinion," Ezell quipped. "These things must be expected in this business."

As large in death as life was rancher Malouf "Oofie" Abraham Sr. When he passed on at age seventy-eight, his grandsons buried him in Canadian with a bottle of Jack Daniels, a wooden nickel Oofie used as a campaign token as a Texas legislator, a pack of cigarettes, and a lighter. But first they ordered the hearse driver to cruise through the rodeo grounds en route to the cemetery. Explained Oofie's son: "They knew their granddaddy would want to make the drag one last time."

After historian J. Evetts Haley first visited Charles Goodnight in the Panhandle, he wrote, "I hesitatingly crossed his ranch-house yard to face the flow of tobacco juice and profanity." Those habits, Haley recalled, concealed Goodnight's "most sensitive nature."

Haley, a rancher himself, wrote the first version of *Charles Goodnight: Cowman and Plainsman* in 1936 and kept revising it for thirteen years. By 1989, it had undergone eleven printings and was said to be the best book ever written about a Texan. His description of Goodnight's 1929 funeral stands as a classic: "His bow-legged gray-headed JA cowboys lowered his massive casket into the grave, and with tears streaming down their leathery, wind-carved faces, shoveled the dirt that covered him up. And there in the graveyard . . . came to rest at last this dominant, driving restless plainsman." Haley also ran unsuccessfully for Texas governor in 1956 and created a flap when he wrote *A Texan Looks at Lyndon: A Study of Illegitimate Power* after LBJ went to the White House.

Although political power shifted to the big cities in Texas, a cotton farmer from tiny Hale Center bucked the trend in the 1990s. Pete Laney, a Democrat, reigned as House Speaker for several terms, even retaining his post when Republicans swept statewide elected offices in 1998. "He is a bipartisan leader and I consider him a friend," said the GOP's top man, Governor George W. Bush.

During the economic uncertainty of the 1980s, the Panhandle's Catholic bishop raised a stir when he suggested Christians at the Pantex nuclear plant reconsider their

Otis Harmon waves to passersby from his wheat field near Tulia. Son-in-law Tommy Womack is in the background.

Windmill sunset, Armstrong County

Panhandle autumn. Cottonwoods near Canadian

employment. Another headache for Pantex was prairie dogs. A spokesman said their web of tunnels penetrated the plant's more secure areas and set off alarms "so we had to cull them out." The critters were shipped to a nature preserve in Fort Worth.

A year after Oprah Winfrey won her mad cow lawsuit brought against her by Panhandle cattlefeeders, a group called People for the Ethical Treatment of Animals erected a billboard in Amarillo that said "Jesus Was a Vegetarian." Then an anonymous prankster telephoned the Society for the Prevention of Cruelty to Animals, threatening to kill a cat a day until the sign came down.

Entrepreneur T. Boone Pickens fought the newspaper in Amarillo on several fronts in the 1980s and later left town. The city missed his company's hefty payroll, but it didn't appear to miss him all that much.

Byron Price, who once ran the sprawling Panhandle-Plains Historical Museum on the campus of West Texas A&M, says, "The people came out here to conquer the land, but only made an uneasy peace with it. It's a hard land. But our people are a strong, hardy bunch and they have a lot of staying power."

Writer Jay Milner finished high school in Lubbock, but retained vivid memories of growing up in the Panhandle in the 1930s. "Mother cooked and cleaned, sewed all the family's clothes, and washed the laundry by hand on a scrub board," he recalls. "Sometimes in winter, when she hung the wash out to dry on the line behind the house, it was frozen stiff by the time she got the clothespins in place."

Crosbyton's concert band, early 1900s

Downtown Plainview in its early days

 y earliest memories are set in Cotton Center, where there was only the gin my father had built, our house and a general store. If there were any other buildings, I don't remember them. You could see for miles in every direction.

The Texas Panhandle is not overrun with people today, but it was even more sparsely populated back then . . .

Daddy and his truck driver, an amiable man everybody called "Brub," often cut across the prairie, ignoring the roads, when they needed to drive to Plainview in a hurry. There was nothing to speak of in the way.

Jay Dunston Milner, *Confessions of a Maddog*, 1998

A couple of good, long, deep breaths of this early, sunny-morning, Mexican border air and God and the devil, both, couldn't trick me into being sad.

Woodie Guthrie, praising Big Bend

20

Near a washboard road on the backside of Big Bend National Park are the remains of a primitive dwelling, no more than a hovel. A desert squatter lived there for decades—some say until he was more than a hundred years old. The nearest water was a half-day's walk to the Rio Grande.

In the same region, there is a dot on the official Texas Department of Transportation highway map for the village of Casa Piedra. One problem: there is no road to Casa Piedra.

The Big Bend Telephone Company had about ninety miles of line in 1997 to serve one customer. "To put it in perspective, I tell people it's like making a local call in Austin and getting a dial tone out of Waco," said Don Richards, an attorney representing the company.

At traffic-choked border crossings from Brownsville to El Paso, drug dogs sniff for contraband, and movements are scrutinized with high-tech precision. At Boquillas in the Big Bend, a crude little rowboat ferries an occasional tourist from the U.S. to the town's cantina on the other side without government interdiction.

If West Texas is a land of contrasts, the mightiest are in the Big Bend. The hottest place is Presidio; the coolest, Marfa. The Big Bend National Park has the Chisos Mountains, river gorges, black bear, a vast desert, and a verdant flood plain among its thousand square miles, most of which are impenetrable.

Alpine may have the state's best baseball park, cozy Kokernot Field, commissioned years ago by the Kokernot ranching family. Alpine itself is the county seat of Brewster County, which is bigger than the state of Connecticut.

The distances are unfathomable to outsiders. An editor in New York had a brainstorm when a horse named Marfa contended for the Kentucky Derby. How about dropping by the town of the same name for reaction, he told a subordinate in Dallas. Little did the New Yorker know he could cross the Atlantic in less time.

Marfa's original reputation was staked on its mysterious naturally occurring lights, which have as yet no explanation. Later came the El Paisano Hotel, where the stars of Hollywood stayed during the filming of *Giant.*

All over the Big Bend, the nighttime's canopy of real stars, with no ambient city light, is inspirational. So is the silence. No wonder an Air Force scheme to practice low-level maneuvers is cause for revolt. The Big Bend is the most pristine part of Texas. Yet, by 1996, pollution from hundreds and

Cathy Fulton sips coffee on a Big Bend Ranch State Park cattle drive.

perhaps thousands of miles away cut visibility on some days by as much as sixty percent.

There are some times where the law is no law at all. A sheriff lost his spurs when he was linked to a horse trailer full of cocaine at the local fairgrounds. Fierce mob warfare was waged in the 1980s on the streets of Ojinaga, just across the border from Presidio.

The law has long arms, though. A big city girl from El Paso missed a turn on a mountain road returning from the chili cook-offs in Terlingua. She survived, but her car was flattened. She returned a few days later to discover authorities had tagged the wreck at the bottom of a canyon for a parking violation.

General Black Jack Pershing chased the bandit revolutionary Pancho Villa across the Rio Grande, but didn't catch him. The splintered remnants of Black Jack's Big Bend camp are still visible on a stone-strewn, uninhabited tabletop mesa.

Before Pancho Villa, the U.S. Army was more successful in combating the Mescalero Apache at a place we now know as Fort Davis. One reason was "Indian Emily." According to local lore, Emily was a comely Apache who was wounded in a raid, rescued, and nursed to health by the mother of an Army lieutenant. She worked for the woman, but secretly fell in love with the lieutenant. When he became engaged to the daughter of another officer at the fort, Emily disappeared. That is, until one night when a guard spied a figure coming toward him in the Big Bend darkness. When the figure failed to respond to his command, the soldier fired. Indian Emily died, but not before she warned of a dawn raid by the Apache.

137

Fort Davis had other distinctions. It was a base for the famed African-American buffalo soldiers, so named by Native Americans because of their curly hair. Also curious were the strange, hump-backed animals—camels—that were an experiment of the U.S. Secretary of War. The secretary, by the way, was Jefferson Davis, and the fort was his namesake. The name stuck, even though he turned Confederate in the American Civil War.

On July 31, 1891, the last troops marched out of town, the region having been declared safe for the vast ranches that were beginning to form.

More than a century later, visitors were still learning that "safe" is a relative term. Cliff-top snipers attacked rafters on a placid stretch of the Rio Grande. Elsewhere, a hungry cougar assaulted a mom who was photographing her three children on a popular Big Bend hiking trail. "I knew that I was probably going to die protecting my children," Mary Jane Coder told the *Valley Morning Star* of Harlingen, Texas, in 1998. Armed only with a pocket knife, she backed the cat down before it took a swipe and bloodied her hand. It continued stalking the quartet on a harrowing two-mile trek back to their car.

Because of such wild animals, the *Texas State Travel Guide* warns pet owners not to leave pets unattended in Big Bend National Park, recommending, "It's best to leave your pets at home."

The Window, Chisos Basin, Big Bend National Park

With the Apaches subdued, the biggest threat to tranquility in the early 1900s was the ongoing conflict between Mexican raiders on one side and ranchers, U.S. cavalry, and Texas Rangers on the other. One such confrontation is described in a slender volume entitled *Circuit Riders of the Big Bend* by W. D. Smithers. Oddly enough, Smithers's intent was to memorialize the preachers, the circuit riders who tended their flocks on ranches too remote for regular attendance at Sunday services.

One Church of Christ minister, the Reverend H. M. Bandy, and his wife were invited to spend Christmas Day 1917 on the Brite Ranch about thirty-five miles west of Marfa. A Mexican contingent of perhaps forty riders had other plans. Coming from the village of Pilares on the other side of the Rio Grande, they hit the Brite Ranch at daybreak. The ranch foreman's father, Sam Neil, grabbed his rifle and began shooting, apparently killing the raiders' leader. The raiders then intercepted the mail stage and executed its three occupants. During a standoff, Reverend Bandy's contingent arrived and was allowed to proceed inside. Years later, Neil's niece, Lela Weatherby, described what happened next in a first-person story in the weekly *Alpine Avalanche:* "Brother Bandy gave a prayer and asked for a gun. My uncle took a long drink of whiskey which caused my Aunt Janie to get on him. But Brother Bandy said, 'No, Sarah Jane, if ever a man needed a swig of whiskey, it is now.'"

Neil vowed never to surrender, and he didn't, even after the raiders took a small boy hostage. But the ranch lost its prized horses and supplies from the ranch storehouses. The raiders retreated with their booty when another rancher, coming for his mail, spotted them and raced away in his car to warn others. In an echo of the Old West, a Christmas Day posse was formed. It included a caravan of cars as well as horses. Cowboys, soldiers from border garrisons, Texas Rangers, and other volunteers laid plans to invade Mexico despite standing orders to the contrary from Washington, D.C. and Austin.

"The bandits and their cohorts in Pilares were asleep when the killing began," said historian Smithers. Perhaps thirty-five male residents of Pilares were slain, whether they participated in the Brite Ranch raid or not. After an investigation by Austin, the Texas Ranger company was officially dissolved—Smithers sniffed—"because eight of them did what they should have done." The violence didn't end there. With some justification, the Americans thought the dismissal of the Rangers would encourage more raids. Only three weeks into the new year, Mexican raiders avenged the Pilares invasion with the killing of a Big Bend rancher's eighteen-year-old son. In renewed pursuit, American troops thwarted an ambush at a border crossing and stormed into Mexico again. They found the dead son's leggings, a boot, and other personal effects. They "then destroyed all the houses," wrote Smithers, "and for a long time there was no more village of Pilares."

So much for Bibles and bullets in the Big Bend, but a vestige of the circuit riders continues to this day. A Presbyterian minister named William B. Bloys organized the Big Bend's first camp meeting in 1890. By the 1930s, the annual event was drawing thousands of worshippers. Not to be outdone, the Baptists began the Paisano Camp Meeting in 1920. Their patron was rancher H. L. Kokernot Sr., who fed the multitudes with meat from his own herds.

The disbanded Ranger troop was another story. According to W. D. Smithers, some of the ex-Rangers helped form a new company "and most served until January 1920 when the U.S. Prohibition Law went into effect. Some of those Rangers had no desire to help enforce that law and they resigned."

That's our Rangers.

Santa Elena Canyon, Big Bend National Park

If people in West Texas's Panhandle had to make an uneasy truce with the land, the land itself sometimes wins outright in the Big Bend. Call it a real life fatal attraction.

A cotton speculator made a crop or two on the slender, fertile plain next to the Rio Grande and even erected a gin. His marketing plan, however, was flawed because there was no nearby market. Nature long ago reclaimed the speculator's fields.

Until recently, Study Butte was a pleasant ghost town, like its Big Bend mining twin Terlingua. Some resettlement has occurred, but there is no hope for a return to the million-dollar heydays when mercury was discovered.

The silver mine at Shafter, named after Colonel "Pecos Bill" Shafter, operated night and day for almost sixty years. Today, nothing's left of the town's fifteen hundred residents but a cemetery.

Highways still are seldom traveled, the perfect metaphor being the opening of a quaint movie called *Dancer, Texas Pop. 81.* Four high-school buddies lounge in sun chairs in the middle of the road outside town, able to see an oncoming car miles away. Fort Davis was the real-life backdrop for *Dancer,* and the bit players were all too real to be actors.

Neither could a movie producer make up the life of Joe Don Looney. A 230-pounder with sprinter's speed, he came out of Paschal High School in Fort Worth and turned heads as a white athlete at tiny, predominantly black Cameron Junior College in Oklahoma. Transferring to Oklahoma University, he ran sixty-two yards from scrimmage on his first carry and a legend was born. Perhaps the most enigmatic football player ever, he left the Sooners after decking an assistant coach. His pro career with five teams was no different. He once refused to carry a play into the game, telling the coach to call Western Union if he wanted a messenger.

Looney cited breach of contract, rather than conscientious objection, when his National Guard Unit was activated during the Vietnam War. He went AWOL for twenty-five days, but eventually served nine months, guarding a fuel depot. He became a vegetarian, meditated in a makeshift pyramid, sought inner peace from India to East Texas, and tried "to fill my day with things I love."

Joe Don's last stop was the Big Bend. He built a solar-heated house near Alpine, where he lived alone without electricity or a telephone. On a morning ride on Texas 118, state police said his motorcycle failed to negotiate a curve, killing him. He was forty-five.

It took eons to create the Big Bend. The evidence is everywhere, from ancient volcanic ash to the skeleton of a colossal flying reptile, the pterosaur, with a wingspan of fifty-one feet.

Whether in prehistoric times or now, survival in the Big Bend has always been tenuous. The white settlers of a century ago displaced the Apaches, fought off the Mexicans, and then put together huge tracts of marginal land to create a ranching economy. Today, their legacy is evident in enormous spreads like the 06, the A. S. Gage Ranch, and the La Escalera, as well as the Trans-Pecos holdings of Clayton Williams and former Texas Governor Dolph Briscoe. But their era is fading, not by bloody revolution but quiet surrender.

The Big Bend is changing because new arrivals want fifty-acre retirement retreats, not fifty-thousand-acre working ranches. At the same time, the federal government is

Deer in a Big Bend meadow

forcing some heirs to peddle their historic holdings because of inheritance taxes. Absentee owners don't want to work the land they inherited. They would rather sell than cope with low prices, taxes, drought, and the economic whims of the cattle business.

At sixty-six, Don McIvor's only option was to put his beloved U Up U Down on the block. "It just became so that I was pretty much the only old ranch left in the Davis Mountains," he told AP correspondent Ed Montes in 1997. "This is not just Jeff Davis County, it's all of West Texas. Marfa, Alpine, they're having the same problems." His remote empire was thirty-nine thousand acres of arid plain, pine-laced hills, and a lush sky island near the higher elevations of 8,378-foot Mount Livermore. It had been in the McIvor family for a century. "Oh, sure, there's a lot of emotion," said McIvor, whose absentee sisters urged the sale. "But I accept them as just emotions. It's the way it came down and I have to accept them or just whimper, and I think it's better to accept them."

The buyer of the U Up U Down was the Nature Conservancy, which proposed to turn Mount Livermore's sky island into a private preserve. Part of the conservation group's plan was to permit ranching on other tracts, but limit development and forbid subdivision. Although his ranching peers were suspicious of the Nature Conservancy's agenda, McIvor believed the plan would preserve the area's heritage. "I'd rather keep it to where it can be ranched a little bit," he said. "That would be my legacy, I guess you might say."

In Marfa, the latest legacy is modern art. As Archer City now has books, Marfa has dozens of giant aluminum boxes, the handiwork of minimalist sculptor Donald Judd. Judd

Autumn in remote McKittrick Canyon, Guadalupe Mountains National Park

Maria Garza and her grandfather cross the Rio Grande near Candelaria, Texas, to shop at San Antonio del Bravo in Mexico.

died in 1994 after twenty years in the Big Bend, leaving his Chianti Foundation to maintain his traditions. It's not unusual for hundreds of artists, critics, groupies, and the plain curious to appear in Marfa for a springtime symposium. The locals say Judd was a tad temperamental but, what the heck, the invasion he inspired has been good for business.

Another kind of invasion hit Fort Davis in the spring of 1997. After Richard McLaren began his Republic of Texas standoff, two hundred reporters, photographers, cameramen, and other media established a foothold at a small rest stop several miles from McLaren's ramshackle compound. Cell phones faded in and out, sunblock was a valuable commodity, and Sunday lunch at the Hotel Limpia was a sellout. The horde booked up the region's

hotels, although the most dedicated journalists huddled in blankets at the media checkpoint for round-the-clock duty during thirty-degree nights.

The standoff ran its course and most of the journalists departed. But one, Mark Babineck of the AP, lingered just long enough to recognize what is special about the Big Bend. "I didn't really notice that big, flawless sky above until after McLaren and most of his ragtag bunch had given up," he said. "I mean, of course, we remarked often on the soul-stirring canvas of constellations that lit our evenings, but we didn't really SEE it until the pressures of the job at hand were relieved. The Hale-Bopp, hardly visible above some smoggy, light-polluted cities, looked like it could drop into the Pecos River at any moment."

Guadalupe Peak is Texas's highest point, another superlative for the Trans-Pecos. Whereas the Big Bend compensates with history and flair, Guadalupe is a brute because of its size.

Its neighbor, Pine Top, is more enticing. Writer Jerry Flemmons journeyed to Pine Top's rim on horseback and then spied McKittrick Canyon, an environmental masterpiece marooned above the endless Far West Texas desert. "The forest is thick in the basin. Fir, ponderosa pine, oak, the red-skinned Texas madrone, a beautiful tree, and stands of maple," he wrote. A "living antiquity," he called it. The Apaches thought McKittrick Canyon was a sanctuary, a place where the mythical gods lived. It's now a part of the Guadalupe Mountains National Park, but probably the Apaches were right.

The Pecos River, briny, often dry, slices through West Texas from New Mexico, providing another rugged layer of definition for the region. It is a narrow and marginal ribbon of life, fed by the winter snows of faraway mountain ranges. By the time it reaches Texas, it's tired.

Like many dreamers before them, a current group of civic leaders believes the world will come to the Trans-Pecos, if only . . .

The latest scheme is an interstate highway terminating at Presidio. They call it *La Entrada al Pacifico,* the idea being the road will connect with the western Mexican port of Topolobampo. Admittedly, said one booster, the trade to justify such a project is "twenty, thirty, forty years down the road."

To the west of the Pecos, the word "sparse" takes on new meaning. Loving County, intersected by the riverbed, is the nation's least populous except for areas of Alaska. There are times you can count the votes in an election on your hands.

The San Solomon Springs at Balmorrhea was an oasis for thirsty buffalo, Indians, and pioneers. Today, the springs feed one of the largest man-made swimming holes in the United States, not far from Interstate 10.

Just as El Capitan in the Guadalupes marked the way for the Spanish and then the Butterfield stage, Guadalupe Peak served as a reference point for the early airline pilots going east and west. It is also said they detoured occasionally to the south to drop packets of mail and newspapers for a rancher who was forty miles from the nearest road.

There is virtually no one living on the thousands of square miles of bone-dry wilderness east of El Paso, although a promoter once hoped the naïve would think so. Neatly engineered "streets" on the desert floor are still visible from an airline window as you approach El Paso from the east. They've been there for years without so much as a single foundation being poured. El Paso is different. Combining its population with its sister Juarez, it might be bigger than Houston.

Clouds shroud the crest of El Capitan in Guadalupe Mountains National Park. Although virtually dry today, the Guadalupe Range is the remains of an ancient marine reef, formed millions of years ago when much of Texas was under water.

West Texas

O beautiful for its cowboy past,
For Big Bend, bold and vast,
For Bob Wills, Boys Ranch, and Big Spring,
El Paso and Abilene.
O West Texas, O Rio Grande,
Brazos, Pecos, and Red;
Caprock's rise, Palo Duro's span,
Where plains and sky are wed.

J.L.

The bones of men and buffalo were gone; the land took them, and remained.

T. R. Fehrenbach, *Lone Star*

21

If there's a special place in heaven for West Texans, Watkins "Watt" Matthews is there, for sure. The model of a West Texas cattleman, he lived on his family's Lambshead Ranch outside Albany until his death in 1997 at ninety-eight. His only extended absence was when he attended Princeton University. At his death, a newspaper headline said: "Die? This epitome of the Texas rancher? How could he?" Rick Perry, Texas commissioner of agriculture, said, "He treated men like men, women like ladies, loved children and the land . . . We lost an extraordinary link to our past." Mused Watt's old pal Dub Bizzell: "He was as good a cowman as they come . . . He could look a cow in the butt and read its mind."

And Frenchy McCormick, the mysterious belle of Tascosa? Given her lusty reign in the frontier Panhandle boomtown, Frenchy wasn't an obvious candidate for the celestial hereafter. But her story of grace came long after her husband Mack's casino closed and the county seat moved elsewhere. As Tascosa shriveled, the McCormicks remained in their two-room adobe home near the Canadian River and hunted the plentiful wild game at their doorstep. "Mack and I discussed the fact that we had lived somewhat on the seamy side, and then he took both my hands in his and we pledged to stick to each other and to the town of Tascosa," she said years

after he died. By then, she was the sole resident of the town. She survived the Dust Bowl years, massive floods, rattlesnakes, and bitter cold on her own. She finally consented to move to the town of Channing only if she could be buried near Tascosa next to Mack. And so she was, carrying the secret of her true identity to the grave.

Enter Cal Farley, a wrestler by profession and a "swindler in the kindest sort of way." Farley, who retired from the sport in the 1930s, formed the Maverick Club to steer troubled boys away from Amarillo's street life through athletics. Farley fretted he was missing the "bottom ten percent," and from that concern emerged the concept of Boys Ranch. The Blivins ranching empire donated 120 acres on the site of the Tascosa ghost town while, according to a friend, Farley "swindled" his way into Amarillo's pockets for contributions to start the project. A story from the 1940s says it all. Three brothers, ages five, ten, and fourteen, arrived by bus at the ranch, each with a tag around his neck. The tag read: "Deliver to Boys Ranch, Amarillo, Texas."

Cal collapsed and died in 1967 while attending Sunday services at the ranch chapel. He was seventy-two.

Another famous West Texan was Dory Funk of the wrestlin' Funk family, who doubled as the Boys Ranch superintendent and

Rancher Watt Matthews, far left, branding cattle at Lambshead Ranch, April 1958

Watt Matthews, 1899–1997

football coach for three years. Dory patented the "spinning toehold" long before TV made the current crop of Hulk Hogans international heroes. Two sons, Terry and Dory Jr., joined the family business, even tag-teaming occasionally in their self-appointed roles as the "good guys."

A mom with a critically ill son asked sports writer Burle Pettit of the *Lubbock Avalanche-Journal* to contact Dory, the boy's idol, on her behalf. To Pettit's surprise, Funk flew his private plane from the family compound at Umbarger and went straight to the hospital, on one condition: no newspaper story. For two hours, Dory regaled the child with tales of his villainous opponents, miraculous escapes, and dramatic conquests. Pettit, sensing a great story, asked Dory to change his mind about a column. "Burle," Dory said, "you think this wrestling is a fake, but I do enough of it straight up that you'll regret it if you write a word."

James Roberts was a World War II hero who returned to the desert town of Andrews and never left—except to purchase newspapers all over Texas. Many of his business decisions were made under a lone spreading elm tree on the highway between Andrews and Lamesa. "Meet me at the tree," he would say to Walter Buckel, his associate in Lamesa. After Roberts died in 1997, citizens of both towns put a plaque by the tree, and they buried him underneath a cluster of elms in Andrews's Old Cemetery.

Wealth came unexpectedly for Missouri Matilda Nail Cook, whose family ranched the Indian Territory before it was Oklahoma. Her brothers bought land near Albany in the early 1900s and asked her husband to join them. She was a widow, childless, and sixty-seven years old in 1925 when wildcatters moved on to her land with few clues about its geology. Their caravan bogged down in mud, so they drilled on that spot. It was a gusher. Instead of leaping into a life of luxury, she used her newfound fortune to create a hospital for working women of her era. It was the

forerunner of Cook's Childrens Medical Center in Fort Worth and one of many hospitals, universities, churches, theaters, museums, parks, and nature preserves to benefit from West Texas's black gold.

Though cow boss Lauro Cavazos never lived in West Texas, he had a profound effect on one of its most prominent institutions, Texas Tech University. Lauro was tall, lean, tough and, when necessary, mean. He arrived at the King Ranch as a strapping eighteen-year-old. He lived, worked, married, and died on the South Texas spread. By today's standards, he was under-educated, over-motivated, church-mouse poor, hopelessly loyal, and patriotic to a fault. At his death in 1958, he left a legacy of hard work and high ideals, and five children. "He had such a presence about him," said a daughter-in-law. "He could walk into a room and not speak and everyone would notice he was there. He was very unusual, yet totally natural."

Fate and football led three of Lauro's offspring across the state, where they put their stamp on Texas Tech as indelibly as Lauro did on the King Ranch. Bobby, an All-American running back, drifted naturally into West Texas ranching. Larry, an educator, returned as president of Texas Tech, and later served as U.S. Secretary of Education. The third, Dick, a military student, became a genuine war hero, heading the U.S. Army Forces Command as a four-star general.

Although the vaquero's life was in his blood, Lauro moved his family to a small house in Kingsville when a daughter approached high school age. His sons later saw the logic—the house was two blocks from an elementary school, one block from Texas A&I College and within walking distance of the high school.

In 1941, Lauro made an eventful foray into West Texas. He rode a King Ranch mare named Catarina to first place in the cutting horse competition at the Texas Cowboy Reunion in Stamford. Catarina beat out the favorite, a legend named Snooks, ridden by

Cow boss Lauro Cavazos, circa 1940

cutting horse king Grady Blue. Lauro also was in the last major gunfight in South Texas, called the Battle of Norias. He fought off bandits from Mexico who attacked a King Ranch camp. His face was on posters in Mexico with a bounty—$25, dead or alive. The low price irritated him mightily.

She came from the East, mainly New York and Virginia. She clashed with the Amarillo school board, and her tenure was abbreviated. Nonetheless, Georgia O'Keeffe's West Texas experience may have changed the face of American modern art. "This is my country; terrible winds and wonderful emptiness," she said. As art director for Amarillo public schools, O'Keeffe ignored the sanctioned text.

"She thought it would be easier for the students to draw objects they were familiar with, and even permitted a boy to bring his pony into the classroom as a model," wrote author Elizabeth Montgomery in *Georgia O'Keeffe*.

O'Keeffe parted ways with Amarillo's educational establishment in the summer of 1913, but she would return to the Panhandle three years later to oversee the art department at what is now West Texas A&M in Canyon. Her surroundings would inspire her to begin a series of watercolors, including the so-called *Blue* series. During her second stay in the Panhandle, she visited Santa Fe, New Mexico, and ultimately settled near there. Her paintings are a testimony to the space and light of the West, and a friend described her as a woman "who lives fearlessly, reasons illogically, who is modest, unassertive and spiritually beautiful . . . "

She would've made a good West Texan.

No man could herd Texas cattle and still be a Christian. There are some things that are morally impossible.

Las Vegas, N.M., *Daily Optic*, October 16, 1883

22

It's not always easy to tell saints from sinners in West Texas. Consider convict-turned-civic godfather Pinkie Roden, who won an award from lawyers for best upholding our system of justice. One journalist's theory is that Pinkie chose the perfect place to settle. "West Texans don't tend to hold a lot of grudges against mavericks," said Ken Brodnax. "They tend to look at what you've done lately."

Maybe that's why Sonny Keesee kept getting elected sheriff in Lubbock County. Some of the rotund lawman's escapades were made for a TV sitcom. County commissioners cut his expense account because he tarried too long on a business vacation to Las Vegas. A prisoner escaped the county jail while he was gone. He once traveled to the capital in Austin to stand up for a couple of boyhood pals who wanted to open a bar. Trouble was, the Lubbock County D.A. was already there to oppose the license. When Sonny died, the county judge said, "The traditional West Texas sheriff has been viewed as a tough, tobacco-chewing, gun-on-the-hip redneck. Sonny was a country boy. He had the guns and the badge, but he was a big teddy bear."

Raul Flores, sheriff of Reeves County for sixteen years, was the stuff of legends—born in a dugout, shining boots in a cathouse at age seven, playing football for Bear Bryant at Texas A&M, and gunning down bandits as a young deputy. At least he said so. "Robin Hood or robbin' hood?" the *Pecos Enterprise* wondered. On his $16,250 annual salary, Sheriff Flores drove a Cadillac and a Lincoln and lived in a sixty-five-thousand-dollar home. The Internal Revenue Service nicked him—a bookkeeping problem, he explained—and his constituents kept returning him to office by landslide margins. That is, until he was hexed by a Mexican witch named Josafina from the border town of Ojinaga. According to Raul, "the spell of death was killing me" before he was healed by a remedy of a silver dollar and a clove of garlic. By then, he'd lost support and finally was unseated in 1992 by a former deputy. "I know how Christ felt," he said shortly before his death. "Christ was persecuted and crucified by the people he loved and served because he was different."

John Tower, the father of the Texas Republican Party, sinned and paid dearly for it.

C. W. Stubblefield, 1994

But, after all, it happened in Washington, D.C., where "they do indeed shoot the wounded," said fellow Texan and former U.S. House Speaker Jim Wright. Tower was a professor at Midwestern State University in Wichita Falls when he decided to take on Lyndon Johnson, who was running simultaneous campaigns for vice president and for the U.S. Senate. "My name is Tower, but I don't," he said, referring to his diminutive stature. Although his hometown newspaper didn't endorse him, Tower collected a surprising forty-one percent of the vote in a losing effort. He became the first GOP senator from Texas since Reconstruction when he upset a Democrat in a special election for the seat that LBJ relinquished to become John Kennedy's vice president.

Campaigning in West Texas in his trademark Savile Row suits, Tower was chided by a supportive rancher, "Son, you're the worst looking candidate I've ever seen." At a fundraiser, another rancher asked, "Are you the little S.O.B. we elected?" And it was the same John Tower whose campaign airplane was forced to land on a farm road during a violent thunderstorm. Unaffected, he instructed the pilot to taxi to the nearest town, where he found a beer hall and began hustling votes.

Tower lasted six terms in Washington's shark-filled waters, becoming the Senate's number one power broker for the nation's military. He angered opponents, consumed his share of Johnny Walker Black, and chased a skirt or two. When President George Bush nominated him for defense secretary, leaks about his private life could have filled an ocean. Responded Tower: "Misstatements, lies, gossip, half-truths, and personal opinion were jumbled together and disseminated by the news media . . . This whirligig spun out of control, and it became a perpetual-motion machine pumping poison into the political process." He lost the nomination and then died tragically in a plane crash while on a book tour. The book contained a dedication

Mural of the late rock-n-roll singer Buddy Holly and his band, the Crickets, in Lubbock.

Holly was born in Lubbock in 1936 and quickly rose to stardom after he developed what he and a teen-aged friend called "Western Bop." His songs are part of music history—"That'll Be the Day," "Peggy Sue," "Maybe Baby," "Oh Boy!" He and the Crickets performed at Harlem's Apollo Theater after promoters mistook their sound for an African-American group. Holly's career ended prematurely when he, Ritchie Valens, and J. P. "The Big Bopper" Richardson were killed in a winter plane crash near Clear Lake, Iowa. He was 22.

to his first wife Lou that said, in part, "She forgave my transgressions and was always constant . . . And in the hour of my travail, she held my hand and said, 'You know I've always believed in you.'"

C. W. Stubblefield was a saint to the greats and not-so-greats who visited his east Lubbock eatery. Stubb's Barbecue was a mecca for the likes of Stevie Ray Vaughan, Joe Ely, and Tom T. Hall. Muddy Waters, John Lee Hooker, the Fabulous Thunderbirds, all played in the shotgun-shack restaurant. Dolly Parton, Willie Nelson, Johnny Cash, and Linda Ronstadt all knew the friendly former Army cook. Stubb died in 1995, but jars of sauces and pickled jalapeños still bear his nickname, as does a café just off Sixth Street in Austin.

"People are good all over, least ways more of them good than bad," he once observed. Rest in peace, Stubb.

The typical Texan is big and breezy, fond of strong language and strong drink.

LIFE Magazine, 1939

23

West Texas farm boy Doyle Brunson was a state champion miler at Sweetwater and a star basketball player at Hardin-Simmons, but his athletic career was cut short by a severely broken leg. So he became a world-class gambler. He was selling business machines in Fort Worth when he stumbled onto a poker game in a customer's office. He won a month's salary, quit his job, and waded into the treacherous world of professional gambling. Known around the world by his nickname "Texas Dolly," Brunson has his headquarters in Las Vegas, where he is recognized by colleagues as the greatest no-limit poker player of all time. Says Dolly: "The only time money means anything to me is when I run out of it."

Folks around Lubbock called Robert Walker "Daddy Warbucks," or just Bucks, and two generations of Texas sports writers loved him like a father. Right up until his death, he was the ultimate Texas Tech booster. Bucks, who was a bit like an affectionate but unruly bear, had a heart bigger than West Texas and a pocketbook to match, and he kept both open most of the time. Some credited him with inventing the concept of television's instant replay, but that was probably part of the Warbucks myth. For real was his annual media golf tournament, the Daddy Warbucks Invitational, known fondly and appropriately as the DWI.

Be it Dolly, Pinkie, or Bucks, the "typical" Texan in the eyes of the outside world very well could be a West Texan. James Dean as Jett Rink in *Giant*. Paul Newman in *Hud*. Cybill Shepherd and Ben Johnson in *The Last Picture Show*. Even Jon Voight's Joe Buck in *Midnight Cowboy*.

In fact, when Don Graham, author of *Cowboys and Cadillacs: How Hollywood Looks at Texas*, selected the ten best Texas movies for *The Dallas Morning News*, the top four struck West Texas themes. "To Hollywood," Graham said, "Texas was the ultimate West, the place of empire, where men who were bigger than life carved kingdoms out of the wilderness. Texas was where the cowboys lived." And, he added, "That's why everybody outside of Texas thinks the whole landscape here is a sprawling dusty plain where the main activity is raising cattle and maybe—as in *Giant*—drilling oil wells."

About *Giant,* the top selection, the *News's* Bryan Woolley wrote: "The great Wide-screen National Movie of Texas, about the metamorphosis of Texas Cattle Kingdom to Oil Empire. Rock Hudson is the cattle king, James Dean the oil baron, Liz Taylor the woman loved by both." Number two was *The Last Picture Show*—"anti-*Giant,*" as Woolley put it. Next was *Red River,* about which Woolley said, "John Wayne becomes everybody's Texan." And, at number four, *Hud,* in which

"McMurtry and Paul Newman kill off the cattle kingdom myth." West Texans all, even if only in the eyes of Hollywood.

Speaking of entertainers, would Buddy Holly's rock 'n' roll have been so unique without a Lubbock twang? How much of the West Texas town of Wink did Roy Orbison carry with him on the way to stardom? Waylon Jennings, who grew up in Littlefield, still sings with at least a hint of West Texas in his repertoire. So it is with country-rocker Joe Ely, who once told a *Dallas Morning News* reporter: "My real inspiration was those old dusty plains. I'd go out and see the beautiful beaches and palm trees in California, but it didn't give me anything to write about. I'd come back to Lubbock, jump in a car, drive fifty miles across those flatlands and I had written three songs."

West Texas wordsmiths write books when they don't sing. There's San Angelo's Elmer Kelton and Abilene's A. C. Greene. Larry L. King, who wrote *Best Little Whorehouse* about another part of Texas, is from Putnam. Janice Woods Windle, author of *True Women,* is from El Paso.

The most revered cowboy poet in 1999 was really a cowgirl, Nessye Mae Roach, whose 1920s childhood was on her parents' ranch near Big Lake and whose courtship with husband J. A. was on horseback. She once wrote about "the sounds of the evening breeze / And the plaintive cattle call." Then she could hear "Daddy strip the last milk from the cow. / 'Twas his last chore of the day. / And Momma completed her work at last, / When she put the milk away."

Doña Sarah Ramirez Nuñez spoke with her recipes, first dished out on four tables in a small abobe building in Fort Stockton. When she died fifty years later, Sarah's was the oldest restaurant in the town, still serving what she called "the Spice of Life."

Everyone's heard of the Buick Electra and the Lockheed Electra jet, but not everyone knows the name was inspired by Electra Waggoner Biggs, an heir to the Waggoner Ranch fortune. Not only rich and stylish, she became an accomplished sculptor. An example of her work is the bronze statue of Will Rogers on his horse Soapsuds outside the Will Rogers Memorial Center in Fort Worth. She sculpted the statue, *Riding into the Sunset,* when she was eighteen.

The work of Lubbock's Glenna Goodacre will be far more widespread after her bust of Sacagawea is minted on the new dollar coin in the year 2000. She also created the bronze *Vietnam Women's Memorial.*

The low-income neighborhood of Ysleta fronts Alameda Avenue in El Paso, home to the amazing 1992 senior class of Ysleta High School. Simultaneously accepted at the prestigious Massachusetts Institute of Technology were Albert Martinez, David Villarreal, Enrique Arzaga, Alicia Ayala, and Liliana Ramirez. The MIT Five "gave a lot of momentum to the school and the community," said counselor Irma Sanchez. "These kids were all motivated."

When small-town prosecutor Albert Valadez was re-elected in 1996, Richard McLaren, leader of the separatist Republic of Texas clan was a free man and full of mischief. A year later, Valadez would convict McLaren for kidnapping charges for the Republic's ill-conceived but widely publicized Big Bend standoff.

In another high-profile case, he and his assistants investigated the controversial death of Esequiel Hernandez Jr., who was tending his goats near the border community of Redford when he was killed by a U.S. Marine on drug surveillance. Despite the national fascination with the Republic of Texas, Valadez said the trial of McLaren and pal Robert Otto was not the most significant in his career. "I don't want to give them the credit."

The world watched when baby Jessica emerged from a well in Midland, 1987.

In October 1987, the nation's attention was riveted on West Texas for fifty-eight incredible hours. That's how long it took to rescue baby Jessica from a well in Midland. Playing in the yard while her mother answered the phone, little Jessica McClure was a year old when she plunged twenty-two feet into an abandoned well surrounded by a layer of super-hard rock. The world watched via television as a rescue crew and citizen volunteers frantically dug a shaft parallel to the one that entrapped Jessica. Finally, two paramedics wiggled into the passageway, slathered the frightened child in petroleum jelly and slid her out into the bright television lights. She lost a toe and bears some minor scars from skin grafts but was described on the tenth anniversary of the ordeal as a child who plays the piano and French horn and zips through her Midland neighborhood on skates. After the near tragedy, sympathetic strangers showered her with teddy bears, gifts, cards, and an estimated one million dollars in cash, which sits in a trust fund awaiting her twenty-fifth birthday. There was even a TV movie: *Jessica: Everybody's Baby.*

Another spunky youngster, Kody Newman of Stanton, won what amounts to the Grand Slam of the stock show set in one spectacular year, 1984. Then fourteen, Kody showed the grand champion steer in livestock competition at Fort Worth, Houston, San Antonio and Denver. Her mom reported in 1998 that Kody, a Texas Tech marketing major, was married, back in Martin County, and training futurity horses for barrel races.

New York City has nothing on West Texas when it comes to precocious little girls. Whereas Eloise roamed the halls of Manhattan's Plaza Hotel in the children's literary classic, there's now a book called *Maggie at the Gage*. Maggie is the real-life daughter of Laurie Stevens, who managed the historic Gage Hotel in Marathon with her husband Bill. Maggie's Aunt Pat illustrated the delightful tale.

West Texas schoolchildren know by heart the story of Cynthia Ann Parker, who was kidnapped by Comanches as a child and taken to the western frontier. Adopted by an Indian family, she married in the tribe and bore the last great Comanche chief, Quanah Parker. Recaptured by Texas Rangers near Crowell at age thirty-four, she languished and died four years later.

Finally, there's the female described by writer Jerry Flemmons. He claims it was a non-Texan—briefly but memorably married to a rancher's daughter—who came up with the perfect definition of a West Texas woman:

On Saturday night she straightens the Picasso on her living room wall, pats her silver blonde hair, takes a final look in the mirror and then drives in her Mercedes to the Lubbock Country Club.

She is dressed in a four-thousand-dollar gold lamé Neiman Marcus dress and an eight-hundred-dollar pair of alligator shoes made exclusively for her by a guy in Rome. At the club, she perches herself on a bar stool, crosses her legs and orders a drink—bourbon with a splash of water . . . Nothing touches her for poise and beauty. Class, wealth and breeding, that's her.

Then she takes out a solid gold cigarette case from her five-hundred-dollar hand-beaded clutch purse, puts the cigarette to her lips and . . .

She'll reach into the purse again, take out a kitchen match, and run the match across her gold lamé hip to light it—and that . . . that's a West Texas woman.

Epilogue

The yips and yells of the cowhands, the random crackle of a forty-five spitting out bullets, the bawling of the thirsty herds, the smell of sweaty leather, the grunt of the bucking bronco, the mail hack dashing up in a cloud of dust—all that's gone. But we've still got sunsets and we've still got courage and we still like folks. And that's all that matters.

Shine Phillips, *Big Spring,* 1942.

So, then, what is West Texas? It *is* the blizzards and the dusters, the tornadoes and the hailstorms, the floods and the marathon dry spells.

It *is* the forts and the ranches and the museums. It *is* the cowboy reunions and the Christmas balls, the oil booms and the oil busts, the wheat fields and the cotton fields, the cows and con-artists. It *is* the mountains, prairies, canyons, farmlands, ranchlands, deserts, and dry creek beds.

It *is* the myths and legends and stories, the buried Cadillacs and prize steers, the lonely windmills and the sizzling ribeyes.

It *is* Muleshoe, Spur and Wink. Happy and Hereford, Quail and Quanah, Buffalo Gap and Buffalo Springs. Era, Earth, Energy and Eden. It *is* Lubbock, Amarillo, El Paso, Odessa, Midland, Abilene, San Angelo, Wichita Falls and, yes, Fort Worth, each the commercial and cultural heartbeat of its own unique province.

It *is* the Big Bend, the Big Country, the Permian Basin, the Panhandle, the High Plains, and at least the western flanks of Texas's matchless paradise, the Hill Country.

West Texas is all this, and more, and like all of America, it is changing. But always it *is* its people, essentially earthy, independent, generous, plain and proud.

Remember Joy Cave, the resolute Guthrie schoolteacher in The Big Empty? Said she: "We don't belong to anybody. We belong to ourselves."

The same might be said of all of West Texas. In *A Personal Country,* A. C. Greene's remembrance of his homeland, there is this observation: "People who do not like West Texas frequently cannot like West Texans. The land is too powerful in them and it is an excessive land."

Believe him.

Moonrise above Texas Highway 170 in Brewster County

Acknowledgments

Without the help of many others, it would be impossible to report on West Texas. We appreciate the publishers, editors, and reporters of the region's newspapers who have provided tips and contributed their stories during the years we have traveled throughout the region.

In writing about West Texas, we also relied on the reporting of other AP journalists like former El Paso Correspondent Eduardo Montes, Lubbock Correspondent Chris Newton, and former Lubbock correspondents Chip Brown, Jean Pagel Yaeger, and Mark Babineck.

We appreciate the culture of AP, which invites reporting that transcends the daily drumbeat of news and permits outside work such as this.

Jerry Flemmons, author of *Texas Siftings,* freely shared his knowledge, notes, and a draft of his newest book on Texas quotations to make this project immensely more entertaining. His encouragement was just as valuable.

Ron Heflin, veteran photojournalist, friend, and now photo editor for the Associated Press in Texas, served as our photographic consultant. Janet M. Neugebauer, associate archivist for Texas Tech University's Southwest Collection, provided the research for historical photographs.

Eileen Lumpkin used the talents she acquired in newspaper reporting and library work to compile the comprehensive index.

The Associated Press's Pat Lantis made AP's photo archive available. The *Fort Worth Star-Telegram, The Dallas Morning News, Lubbock Avalanche-Journal, San Angelo Standard-Times, El Paso Times, Odessa American, Austin American-Statesman, Brownwood Bulletin, Abilene Reporter-News,* the *Times Record News* of Wichita Falls, and *Amarillo Globe-News* gave their permissions for photo use. We especially appreciate *Star-Telegram* photographer Rodger Mallison's contributions as well as the photojournalism of AP's Eric Gay and the work of Joe Don Buckner of the *Lubbock Avalanche-Journal.*

Anne Cook of the Texas Department of Transportation's photo library steered us to many of this book's compelling images. And it was a treat to become acquainted with Wyman Meinzer, photographer of the "Big Lonesome," whose pictures find beauty where others have seldom looked.

We appreciate the support of John T. Montford, chancellor of Texas Tech University, who wrote our foreword. Chancellor Montford also was a resource for his experiences practicing law and representing his district in the Texas Senate. Texas Tech's Cindy

Rugeley and Carole Young were also helpful, as was ex-West Texas journalist Jerry Hall of Austin.

Among newspapers whose files or background we used are the *San Angelo Standard-Times*, *The Pampa News*, *The Hereford Brand*, *Wichita Falls Times Record News*, *Snyder Daily News*, *Fort Worth Star-Telegram*, *The Dallas Morning News*, *Houston Chronicle*, *San Antonio Express-News*, *Abilene Reporter-News*, *Dalhart Daily Texan*, *Pecos Enterprise*, *Plainview Daily Herald*, *Lubbock Avalanche-Journal*, *The Midland Reporter-Telegram*, *El Paso Times*, *Amarillo Globe-News*, *Odessa American*, *Big Spring Herald*, *The Eagle* of Bryan-College Station, *Vernon Daily Record*, and *Brownwood Bulletin*.

Texas Monthly magazine was an additional resource, as was *The Handbook of Texas* produced by the Texas State Historical Association, *Texas from the Frontier to Spindletop* by James L. Haley, and the Texas Department of Transportation's *Texas State Travel Guide*. The *Travel Guide* is an amazing source of the quirky historical facts that help define West Texas.

Also: *Texas* by Jerry Flemmons, *Oil Legends of Fort Worth* by the Historical Committee of the Fort Worth Petroleum Club, *Pioneer Jewish Texans* by Natalie Ornish, *Texas Big Rich* by Sandy Sheehy, and the classic *Charles Goodnight: Cowman and Plainsman* by J. Evetts Haley. These and additional reference sources are identified in the text.

Most especially, we acknowledge not only the text but the inspiration of *A Personal Country* by A. C. Greene, which should be a West Texan's bible. Also, the novels about Gus and Call by Larry McMurtry, and *Lost in West Texas* by the late Jim Corder.

Excerpts from Kent Biffle's column on drought humor reprinted by permission of *The Dallas Morning News*.

Excerpts from Mike Blackman's vignette on traveling from his hometown of Anson, Texas, to the Fort Worth Livestock Show reprinted by permission of the *Fort Worth Star-Telegram*.

Excerpts from Ken Brodnax's column on Bubba Gravelhauler reprinted by permission of the *Odessa American*.

Excerpts from *Oil Legends of Fort Worth* reprinted by permission of the Fort Worth Petroleum Club.

Excerpts from Jay Dunston Milner's reminiscence of growing up in the Texas Panhandle, taken from his book *Confessions of a Maddog*, reprinted by permission of Jay Dunston Milner.

Excerpts from *The Last of the Old-Time Cowboys*, published by Republic of Texas Press, by permission of Wordware Inc.

Portions of *West Texas* first appeared in an essay on West Texas by Mike Cochran and John Lumpkin for The Associated Press in the fall of 1998.

Some anecdotes and profiles in *West Texas* were taken from feature stories by Mike Cochran for The Associated Press from 1970 to 1999.

Photo Credits

(Reference numbers for Texas Department of Transportation and Texas Tech University Southwest Collection archives are in parentheses)

Page

ii-iii Wyman Meinzer, with permission

vii Anonymous, courtesy Southwest Collection (SWCPC 454)

xii Anonymous, courtesy Texas Department of Transportation (7A-West-7)

xiv Roger Mallison, 1998, permission *Fort Worth Star-Telegram*

2 Rodger Mallison, permission *Fort Worth Star-Telegram*

4 Randy Green, courtesy Texas Department of Transportation (15-Cap-18)

5 Rodger Mallison, permission *Fort Worth Star-Telegram*

6 *Top.* Wyman Meinzer, with permission
Bottom. John Lumpkin

8 Eric Gay, permission The Associated Press

9 J. Griffis Smith, courtesy Texas Department of Transportation (7B-Ft.S-1.1)

10 J. Griffis Smith, courtesy Texas Department of Transportation (7B-Bal-7)

11 Rodger Mallision, permission *Fort Worth Star-Telegram*

12 Eric Gay, permission The Associated Press

13 *Top.* Richard Reynolds, courtesy Texas Department of Transportion (7A-ElP-21)
Bottom. Eric Gay, permission The Associated Press

14 Lara Meckfessel, permission *Lubbock Avalanche-Journal*

15 Jack Lewis, courtesy Texas Department of Transportation (15-PDC-56)

16 Rodger Mallison, permission *Fort Worth Star-Telegram*

17 Randy Green, courtesy Texas Department of Transportation (15-Cap-18)

18 Wyman Meinzer, with permission

20 Earl Nottingham, with permission

22 Joe Don Buckner, permission *Lubbock Avalanche-Journal*

25 Randy Green, courtesy Texas Department of Transportation (17A-S.Flat-13)

26 Anonymous, courtesy Southwest Collection (SWCPC 334-E2)

28 Anonymous, permission Panhandle-Plains Historical Museum

32 Evans Caglage, permission *The Dallas Morning News*

33 Randy Green, courtesy Texas Department of Transportation (17A-West-29A)

35 Ron Heflin, permission The Associated Press

37 Family collection, permission Jane Roden

40 Eric Gay, permission The Associated Press

41 Eric Gay, permission The Associated Press

42 Eric Gay, permission The Associated Press

43 David Branch, permission *Brownwood Bulletin*

45 Ron Heflin, permission The Associated Press

46 Frank Reeves, courtesy Southwest Collection (FR 301)

47 *Top.* Rodger Mallison, permission *Fort Worth Star-Telegram*

    Bottom. Bob Parvin, courtesy Texas Department of Transportation (7B-S.Ang-2)

48 Anonymous, courtesy Southwest Collection (SWCPC 291)

49 Joe Don Buckner, permission *Lubbock Avalanche-Journal*

51 Curt Wilcott, with permission

52 Anonymous, courtesy Southwest Collection (SWCPC 147-E4)

53 Anonymous, courtesy Southwest Collection (SWCPC 110-E1)

54 Kevin Stillman, courtesy Texas Department of Transportation (28-Sunset-19)

59 Tim Sharp, permission The Associated Press

60 Rodger Mallison, permission *Fort Worth Star-Telegram*

62 Wyman Meinzer, with permission

63 Ron Heflin, permission The Associated Press

64 Ron Heflin, permission The Associated Press

65 Wyman Meinzer, with permission

67 Ron Heflin, permission The Associated Press

70 John Lumpkin

72 Eric Gay, permission The Associated Press

73 John Lumpkin

74 John Lumpkin

75 Anonymous, courtesy Southwest Collection (SWCPC 587)

76 Rodger Mallison, permission *Fort Worth Star-Telegram*

77 Frank Reeves, courtesy Southwest Collection (FR 265)

78 *Top.* Anonymous, courtesy Southwest Collection (Museum 1971-105-1)

    Bottom. Anonymous, courtesy Southwest Collection (SWCPC 332-E1)

79 *Top.* Anonymous, courtesy Southwest Collection SWCPC 1855-88-22)

    Bottom. Anonymous, courtesy Southwest Collection (SWCPC 460)

80 Poster, courtesy Southwest Collection (SWCPC 587)

83 Kevin Stillman, courtesy Texas Department of Transportation (2D-Groom-1)

85 Anonymous, XIT photo, courtesy Southwest Collection (SWCPC 117-E3)

87 Anonymous, courtesy Southwest Collection (SWCPC 417)

88 Darwin Weigel, permission *Odessa American*

89 Anonymous, courtesy *Lubbock Avalanche-Journal*

90 Anonymous, courtesy Southwest Collection (SWCPC 57(R)E11). Donor: Mrs. Walter Clark

91 Milton Adams, permission *Lubbock Avalanche-Journal*

93 Ron Heflin, permission The Associated Press

96 Eric Gay, permission The Associated Press

97 Anonymous, courtesy Southwest Collection (SWCPC 397-E1)

98 Anonymous, courtesy Southwest Collection (SWCPC 39A E6)

99 Anonymous, courtesy Southwest Collection (SWCPC 397-E3)

101 Jack Lewis, courtesy Texas Department of Transportation (15-PDC-13)

102 Lance Moler, permission *Lubbock Avalanche-Journal*

103 Eric Gay, permission The Associated Press

105 Bob Parvin, courtesy Texas Department of Transportation (28-Lighning-1)

106 Pat Blacklock, permission *Times Record News* of Wichita Falls

109 Jon Frelich, permission The Associated Press and Jon Frelich

114 Family collection, permission Norbert Schlegel

117 Anonymous, courtesy Southwest Collection (SWCPC 147)

118 Anonymous, courtesy Southwest Collection (Heritage Club E101)

121 Ron Heflin

123 Eric Gay, permission The Associated Press

125 Dale Wiseman, courtesy Texas Department of Transportation (15-PDC-69)

126 Anonymous, courtesy Southwest Collection (SWCPC 38(B))

127 Richard Reynolds, courtesy Texas Department of Transportation (14E-Ali-13)

128 John Lumpkin

129 Anonymous, courtesy Southwest Collection (SWCPC 259-E2)

130 Anonymous, courtesy Southwest Collection (SWCPC 356-E2

131 Eric Gay, permission The Associated Press

132 Robert Mulhern, permission *Amarillo Globe-News*

133 Randy Green, courtesy Texas Department of Transportation (16A-57)

134 Anonymous, courtesy Southwest Collection (Museum 55-104-6)

135 Anonymous, courtesy Southwest Collection (Museum 55-130-49)

137 Darwin Weigel, permission *Odessa American*

139 Rodger Mallison, permission *Fort Worth Star-Telegram*

141 Rodger Mallison, permission *Fort Worth Star-Telegram*

143 Rodger Mallison, permission *Fort Worth Star-Telegram*

144 Richard Reynolds, courtesy Texas Department of Transportation (14B-170)

145 Jack Kurtz, permission *El Paso Times*

147 Richard Reynolds, courtesy Texas Department of Transportation (14B-178)

149 Frank Reeves, courtesy Southwest Collection (FR 161)

150 Ken Ellsworth, permission *Abilene Reporter-News*

152 Anonymous, courtesy King Ranch archives

155 Jay Godwin, permission *Austin American-Statesman*

157 Tim Sharp, permission The Associated Press

161 Eric Gay, permission The Associated Press

165 Rodger Mallison, permission *Fort Worth Star-Telegram*

Index

A

Abilene, xi, 8 10, 11, 12, 18, 29, 35, 42, 45, 69, 71, 81, 85, 89, 90, 113, 114, 115, 116, 160, 163
Abilene Christian College, 89
Abilene Reporter-News, 25, 18, 90, 167, 168
Abraham, Malouf "Oofie," 130
Adair, John George, 27
Adobe Walls, 124
Albany, 7, 18, 71, 148, 151
Alibates National Monument, 126, 127
Alpine, 2, 50, 136, 142, 144
Alpine Avalanche, 140
Amarillo, 1, 8, 11, 21, 27, 29–30, 31, 32, 71, 73, 84, 86, 95, 108, 116, 122, 134, 148, 153, 163
Amarillo Globe-News, 27, 130, 166, 167
Amistad, 1
Anderson, Donny, 90
Andrews, 151
Anson, 1, 11, 86, 120, 167
Apaches, 39, 137, 140, 142, 146
Applewhite, Marshall Herff, 81
Archer City, 45-48, 90, 144
Aspermont, 63, 64, 91
Associated Press, 57, 166, 167
Austin, v, 3, 23, 27, 29, 36, 37, 40, 44, 50, 122, 127, 136, 140, 154, 158
Austin American-Statesman, 23, 166
Autry, George, 16

B

Babineck, Mark, 145, 166
Badlands, 61
Ballinger, 10, 91
Balmorrhea, 146
Bandy, H. M., 140
Bangs, 81, 82
Barnes, Ben, 40
Barr, Candy, 19, 39, 116
Barry, Janelle, 62, 68
Bass (Nancy Lee and Perry R.) Performance Hall, 120

Baugh, David, 88
Baugh, Sammy, 19, 86, 89, 92–94
Bean, Alan, 21
Bean, Judge Roy, 31, 84
Bemelmans, Ludwig, 6
Benedum, Mike, 55
Benjamin, vii, 18, 62
Biffle, Kent, 100, 167
Big Bend, xii, 1, 2, 9, 11, 12, 19, 20, 50, 61, 81, 136–147, 160, 163
Big Lake, 44, 52, 160
Big Spring, 4, 8, 9, 11, 34, 37, 52, 71, 82, 88, 99, 163
Big Spring Herald, 99, 167
Big Springs Ranch, 80
Biggs, Betty, 127
Biggs, Electra Waggoner, 160
Billie Sol: King of the Texas Wheeler Dealers (Estes), 33
Billy the Kid, 19, 122
Blackman, Mike, 120, 167
Blanket, 92
Blasingame, Tom, 75
Bloys, William B., 140
Boomtown, 9
Borden County, 61
Borger, 28–29, 69, 108, 122, 127
Bovina, 126
Boys Ranch, 1, 74, 148
Brady, v, 7, 28, 33, 35, 39
Brazos River, xi, 63, 66
Breckenridge, 119
Brewster County, 2, 136, 165
Briscoe County, vii
Briscoe, Dolph, 95, 142
Brite Ranch, 140
Brodnax, Ken, 57, 154, 167
Bronco, 44
Bronte, 44
Brownwood, 7, 13, 39–43, 69, 92, 116
Brownwood Bulletin, 166, 167
Brunson, Doyle, 159

Buffalo Gap, 69, 72, 163
Buffalo Springs, 85, 163
Buffalo soldiers, 138
Buffe, Leonard, 92
Burkburnett, 9
Burnett, S. B. "Burk," 56
Bush, George W., 9, 19, 131

C

Cactus, 44
Cadillac Ranch, 31
Canadian, 105, 130, 133
Canadian Record, 130
Canadian River, 1, 122, 148
Canyon, 86, 153
Canyon Reef, 55
Capitol Freehold Land and Investment Co., 27
Caprock, xi, 3, 6, 7, 60, 61, 99, 116
Caprock Canyon, vii–viii, 4, 17
Carpenter, Marge, 82
Carroll, Rusty, 114–115
Carruth, J. W. "Hog Creek," 19
Carter, Amon G., xi, 19, 118 119, 120
Casa Piedra, 136
Castro City, 23
Cavazos, Lauro, 151–153
Chagra, Liz, 108
Charles Goodnight: Cowman and Plainsman, (Haley), 131, 167
Childress, 2, 95
Chisholm Trail, 69, 84, 116, 120, 121
Chisos Mountains, 1, 136, 139
Circle Dot Ranch, 84
Circuit Riders of the Big Bend, (Smithers), 81, 140
Cisco, 11, 60, 119
Cisneros, Henry, 108
Clairemont, 66, 68
Clarendon, 81
Clark, Jim, 44
Claude, 45
Colorado City, 44, 98, 113
Comanches, 3, 19, 39, 124, 162
Concho River, 4, 25, 47, 99
Confessions of a Maddog, (Milner), 135, 167
Connally, John, 40
Coody, Charles, 87
Cook, Missouri Matilda Nail, 151
Corder, Jim ,1, 17, 62,66, 68, 167
Cottle County, 61
Cowboys and Cadillacs: How Hollywood Looks at Texas (Graham), 159
Crenshaw, Ben, 89
Crosbyton, 134
Crow, Kenneth, 114–115
Crowell, 162

D

Daddy's Roommate (Willhoite), 82

Dalhart, 8, 74, 97, 123, 124
Dallas Cowboys, 23, 86, 90
Dallas Morning News, The, 100, 108, 159, 160, 166, 167
Dancer, Texas Pop. 81, 142
Davis Mountains, 21, 144
Davis, Charlie, 42
Davis, Cullen, 29
Davis, Jefferson, 138
Dawn, 126
Dead Man's Walk (McMurtry), 124
Dead Solid Perfect (Jenkins), 88
Dearen, Patrick, 75, 167
Del Rio, xi, xii, 44, 84
Desdemona, 19
Dickens, 68
Dickens County, 61
Dimmit, 23
Double Mountains, 1, 17, 18, 67, 68
Dowlen, George, 30
Draw, 44
Dryden, 44
Duane's Depressed (McMurtry), 48
Dublin, 44
Dumas, 4
Dykes, Spike, 3

E

Eastland, 8, 119
Eden, 44, 163
Edwards, Elva Jo, 38
El Paso, vi, xi, 3, 4, 11, 16, 24, 44, 45, 71, 85, 86, 108, 116, 136, 137, 146, 160, 163, 166, 167
Ely, Joe, 158, 160
Erdmann, Ralph, 111
Estes, Billie Sol, 33–36, 82, 108
Estes, Pam, 33
Expedition Through Unexplored Texas (Parker), 14
Ezell, Ben, 130

F

Farley, Cal, 148
Farwell, Charles, 27
Farwell, John, 27
Fehrenbach, T. R., 77, 148
Fisher County, 18, 61, 115
Fisher, Helen, 69
Flemmons, Jerry, 146, 162, 167, 168
Flores, Raul, 154
Floydada, 81
Flying Queens, 86
Foard County, 61
Fort Concho, 1
Fort Davis, 1, 29, 97, 108, 137–138, 142, 145
Fort Phantom Hill, 1, 12
Fort Stockton, 1, 9, 16, 69, 160
Fort Worth, v, vi, vii, xi, xii, 3, 7, 19, 29, 44, 61, 68, 71, 85, 94, 95, 108, 116, 119–121, 122, 127, 134, 142, 151, 159, 160, 161, 163

Fort Worth stockyards, 69
Fort Worth Star Telegram, 118, 120, 166, 167
Four Sixes Ranch (6666), 1, 68, 108
Franklin Mountains, 4, 147
Franklin, 34
Friday Night Lights (Bissinger), 13, 88
Fritch, 126
Funk, Dory, 148, 151

G

Gage Hotel, 162
Gage, A.S. Ranch, 142
Gainesville, 44
Garza County, 61
Georgia O'Keeffe (Montgomery), 153
Giant (movie), xii, 45, 136, 159
Girvin, 16
Golding, Joe, 92
Goodnight, 126
Goodnight, Charles, xi, 19, 27, 28, 79, 84, 131
Goodnight, Molly, 122
Gordon, 92
Govan, William Henry "H," 91–92
Graham, 9
Graham, Don, 159
Greene, A. C., xi, 14, 61, 160, 163, 167
Greene, Pete, 115
Guadalupe Mountains, 24, 144, 146, 147
Guadalupe Peak, 146
Gunnels, Mary, 108
Guthrie, Woodie, 136
Guthrie, vii, 18, 68, 163

H

Hale Center, 97, 103, 110, 131
Hale Center American, 103
Haley, J. Evetts, 27, 69, 131, 167
Haley, James L., 122, 167
Halff, Mayer, 84
Halff, Soloman, 84
Hamlin, 61, 91
Hank the Cowdog, 1
Happy, 9, 163
Hardin-Simmons University, 159
Harlingen, *Valley Morning Star,* 138
Harrelson, Charles, 108
Harris, David, 108
Harrison, Bob, 42
Haskell County, 61
Haskins, Don, 86
Hawkins, Yisrayl, 81
Haynes, Richard "Racehorse", 29–30, 108
Heather Has Two Mommies (Newman), 82
Heirig, Dick "Two-Gun," 28
Hereford, 26, 95, 116, 124, 126, 128, 163
High Plains, 1, 16, 49, 61, 88, 163
Hinckley, John, 21, 23
Hollandsworth, Skip, 23

Holly, Buddy, 8, 157, 160
Holub, E. J., 90
Horseman, Pass By (McMurtry), 45
House, Boyce, 27
Hud (movie), 45, 159
Hueco Tanks, 11
Hunt, Bunker, 29
Hunt, Herbert, 29
Huntsville, 115

I

I'm from Texas, You Can't Steer Me (Jackson), 44
Impact, 45
Indian Emily, 137
Iraan, 7
Ivins, Molly, 21

J

Jackson, Thomas, 44
Jackson, T. J. "Stonewall," 64
Janca, Adolph, 44
JA Ranch, 74, 75, 131
J. M. Ranch, 84
Jayton, 17, 61, 66
Jayton Chronicle, 66
Jeff Davis County, 144
Jenkins, Dan, 88
Jennings, Waylon, 160
Johnson, Lyndon, 33, 34, 156
Jones County, 61
Jones, Slim, 28
Juarez, Mexico, 4, 13, 146
Judd, Donald, 144–145

K

Kaplan, David, 108
Kaufman, David Spangler, 84
Keesee, Sonny, 154
Kelton, Elmer, 98, 160
Kent County, 61
King County, 61, 62, 68
King, Larry L., 74, 75, 160
King Ranch, 151, 153
Kingsville, 151
Knox City, 68
Knox County, 61, 62
Kohlberg, Olga, 84–85
Kress, 84
Krupp, Haymon, 85

L

La Escalera Ranch, 142
La Tuna (prison), 108
Lake Ivie, 25
Lake Meredith, 1
Lambshead Ranch, 71, 148, 149
Laney, Pete, 131
Langtry, 11, 31, 33

Lariat,44
Lark, 126
Last of the Old Time Cowboys, The (Dearen), 75
Last Picture Show, The (movie), 45, 47, 159
Layne, Bobby, 87
Leatherman, J. D., 56
Lefors, 9
Lenorah, 91
Levelland, 44
Lilly, Bob, 90 119
Littlefield, viii, 160
Llano, 71
Llano Estacado, 11, 45
Lonesome Dove (McMurtry), 45
Lone Star (Fehrenbach), 77, 148
Looney, Douglas, 23
Looney, Joe Don, 142
Loop, 44
Lost in West Texas (Corder), 1, 17, 167
Loving County, 146
Lowake Inn, 69
Lowe, Kenneth, 42
Lubbock, v, vi, vii, xi, 3, 8, 9, 13, 14, 17, 21, 23, 24, 29,
    36, 48, 61, 69, 85, 87, 88–89, 95, 97, 103–104,
    108, 125, 134, 157, 158, 159, 160, 162, 163, 166
Lubbock Avalanche-Journal, 151, 166, 167
Lubbock County, 154
Lucas, Henry Lee, 29
Luskey, Abraham, 85

M

Mackenzie, Ranald, xi, 68
Marathon, 84, 162
Marcy, Randolph, 62
Marfa, 45, 136, 140, 144–145
Marsh 3, Stanley, 19, 31–32, 73
Marshall, Henry, 34
Masterson, Bat, 122
Matador Land and Cattle Co., 27
Matador Ranch, 24, 74, 77, 79
Matthews, Watkins "Watt," 19, 71, 148, 149, 150
McAliffe, Leon, 127
McClellan, Mike, 42
McClure, Jessica, 161
McColloch County, 7
McCombs, Red, 19
McCormick, Frenchy, 122, 148
McCullough, L. H., 58
McIvor, Don, 144
McKittrick Canyon, 144, 146
McLaren, Richard, 21, 29, 145, 160
McMurtry, Larry, 45–48, 124–125, 160, 167
Meinzer, Wyman, 18, 62, 166
Melvin, 27–28
Memphis, 44
Meyer, Dutch, 86, 92
Miami, 44
Michener, James, 50, 52, 60

Midland, 3, 19, 21, 24, 25, 50, 51, 55, 56, 58, 69, 84,
    95, 99, 161, 163
Midland Reporter-Telegram, 24, 57, 95, 167
Miller, Dee, 73
Miller, Tommy, 90
Milner, Jay Dunston, 134, 135, 167
Milner, Kenneth Glenn, 111
Mineral Wells, 1
Mitchell County, 52
Monahans, 7–8
Monahans Sandhills State Park, 3, 6
Montes, Ed, 144, 166
Montford, John T., v–viii, 21, 166
Montgomery, Elizabeth, 153
Morrow, Bobby, 89
Motley County, 61
Muleshoe, 1, 21, 24, 116, 163
Mullin, 92
Munday, 90
Mutscher, Gus, 29

N

Nazareth, 44, 86
Netscape, 44
Newman, Kody, 161
Nieman, Speedy, 124
Norfleet (Norfleet), 110
Norfleet, J. Frank, 110
Norris, J. Frank, 120
Notrees, 44
Nuñez, Doña Sarah Ramirez, 160

O

O'Keeffe, Georgia, 153
Odessa, 1, 4, 8, 9, 13, 19, 21, 24, 36, 37, 38, 54, 58, 85,
    87, 88, 95, 163
Odessa American, 21, 24, 57, 166, 167
O'Donnell, 8
Ogallala Aquifer, 4
Oil Legends of Fort Worth (Fort Worth Petroleum Club
    Historical Committee), 56, 119, 167
Oil Patch, 52, 55
Old Glory, 17, 63–64
Olney, 12, 111
Operation Teacup, 98
Orbison, Roy, 160
Orla, xiv

P

Paducah, 3
Paisano Pete, 1, 9
Paint Rock, 11
Palo Duro Canyon, 1, 14, 16, 17, 68, 75, 101, 122, 124,
    125, 126
Pampa, 71, 124
Panhandle (region), xi, 1, 9, 14, 19, 21, 26, 27, 28, 30,
    32, 44, 58, 71, 73, 77, 81, 84, 86, 99, 112, 116,

122, 124, 125, 126, 127, 131, 133, 134, 135, 142, 148, 153, 163
Panhandle (city), 7, 111, 127
Pantex, 131, 134
Parker, Bruce, 110
Parker, Cynthia Ann, 162
Parker, Doyle, 110
Parker, James Henry, 110
Parker, Quanah, 110, 124, 162
Parker, Raymond, 110
Parker, Tildy, 110
Parker, W. B., 14, 61, 62
Patoski, Joe Nick, 120
Pecos, 24, 29, 33, 34, 69, 71, 74, 82, 89, 97
Pecos Independent and Enterprise, 82, 154
Pecos River, xi, 1, 16, 84, 145, 146
Permian Basin, 24, 55, 58, 61, 85, 163
Pershing, Black Jack, 137
Personal Country, A (Greene), 14, 61, 163, 167
Phillips, 126
Pickens, T. Boone, 134
Pickrell, Frank, 52, 55, 85
Pilares, Mexico, 140
Pine Top, 146
Pioneer Jewish Texans, 84, 167
Pitchfork Ranch, 74
Pitts, Groner, 39–41
Plainview, 2, 25, 44, 84, 86, 135
Plainview Daily Herald, 84, 167
Possum Kingdom Lake, 9, 69
Post, 3, 27
Post, C. W., 27, 99
Powers, Edward, 99
Presidio, 136, 137, 146
Putnam, 160
Pyote, 1

Q

Quail, 126, 163
Quanah, 3, 98, 99, 163
Quien Sabe Ranch, 84
Quitaque, 4

R

Ragtown, 122
Ranger, 52, 56, 57, 117 119
Red River (movie), 159
Red River, 61, 90, 125
Redwine, Booger, 3
Reid, Ace, 1
Reid, Jan, 92
Republic of Texas, 21, 29, 108, 145, 160
Rio Grande, xii, 4, 11, 13, 82, 84, 136, 137, 138, 140, 142, 145
Roach, Nessye Mae, 160
Road Food, 10
Robert Lee, 2
Roberts, James, 151

Roby, vi, 21, 113, 115
Rochester, 17
Roden, Tom "Pinkie," 36–38, 154
Rodriguez, Sammy, 81
Rogers, W. D. "Dub," 21
Rogers, Will, 4, 22, 24, 160
Ropesville, vii
Roscoe, 42
Ross, Sul, 19
Rotan, 19, 21, 91–92, 112, 113, 114
Rude Behavior (Jenkins), 88
Rule, 41, 63

S

Saint's Roost, 81
Salt War, 24
San Angelo, vi, xi, 4–5, 10, 11, 29, 47, 69, 71, 86, 95, 97, 98, 110, 160, 163
San Angelo Standard Times, 20, 69, 166, 167
San Antonio, 19, 44, 161
San Antonio Express-News, 167
San Solomon Springs, 146
Sanderson, 1
Santa Rita No. 1, 44, 50, 55–56, 85
Saragosa, 97–98
Scarborough, Charlie, 115
Schkade, Carl, 56
Schlegel, Jaye Nell, 112-115
Schlegel, Norbert, 112-115
Scurry County, 61
Seminole, 42
Semi-Tough (Jenkins), 88
Seymour, 9
Settles Hotel, 4, 8, 9
Shaftner, 142
Shaid, Orrin, 27–28
Shamrock, 1, 112, 113
Sharp, Marsha, 86
Sharpstown, 29
Sherrod, Blackie, 95
Slaton, 97
Smith, Preston, 29, 36
Smithers, W. D., 81, 140
SMS Ranch, 1, 77
Snyder, 26, 88, 113
Snyder Daily News, 26, 167
Sosa, Gaspar Castano de, 84
South and West Land Company, 80
South Plains, xi, 1, 3, 36, 77, 103, 125
Spraberry Trend, 55
Spur, 3, 19, 44, 62, 68, 81, 163
Spur Ranch, 78
Stamford, 1, 19, 39, 42, 66, 74, 90, 151
Stanton, 161
Star, 44
Steinbeck, John, 7
Stetson (hat), 27
Stevens, Laurie, 162

Stevenson, Coke, Jr., 36, 38
Stillwell, Hallie, xiii, 19, 20
Stinnett, 90
Stonewall County, 61, 63, 64, 67, 68
Strauss, Robert, 19
Strawn, 92
Stubblefield, C. W., 154, 158
Stubbs Barbecue, 158
Stubbs, Bobby, 48
Study Butte, 11, 142
Sweetwater, 2, 10, 69, 92, 113, 159
Swenson, 17, 64
Swenson, Gene, 66
Swenson, Magnus "Swede," 77

Swink, Jim, 119
Swoopes, Sheryl, 14, 89

T

Tahoka, 3, 38
Tascosa, 26, 122, 148
Templin, Bobby, 112–115
Templin, Rhonda, 112–115
Tennyson, 44
Terlingua, 4, 12, 137, 142
Terrell, David, 81, 82–83
Texan Looks at Lyndon, A:A Study of Illegitimate Power (Haley), 131
TEXAS (pageant), 124
Texas (Michener), 52, 60
Texas Almanac, 7, 48, 68
Texas Big Rich (Sheehy), 32, 167
Texas Celebrates (Kaplan), 108
Texas Christian University, 8, 86, 87, 92, 119
Texas Cowboy Reunion, 1, 74
Texas Highways, 17
Texas Monthly, 23, 74, 81, 92, 120, 126, 167
Texas Playboys, 127
Texas Proud, (House), 27
Texas Rangers, 19, 21, 24, 27, 28, 37, 44, 45, 110, 140, 162
Texas Rural Legal Aid (TRLA), 26
Texas Tech University , vi, 3, 13–14, 21–23, 24, 86, 87, 90, 103, 118, 151, 159, 161, 166, 168
Texas Western University, xi, 86
Texasville (McMurtry), 48
Texasville (movie), 47
Thurber, 9, 81
Tiguas, 45
Time It Never Rained, The, (Kelton), 98
Tin Cup, 88
Tower, John, 106, 154, 156
Toyah, 24, 56
Travels With Charley (Steinbeck), 7
True Women (Windle), 160
Tulia, 45, 131
Turkey, 126–127
Tye, 12

U

U Up U Down Ranch, 144
University of Texas, 42, 44, 85
University of Texas-El Paso, 86
University of Texas-Permian Basin, 24

V

Vain Glory (Reid), 92
Valachi, Joseph, 108
Valadez, Albert, 160
Varsity Blues, 3, 88
Vega, 86
Vernon, 44, 46, 76
Villa, Pancho, 19, 137

W

Waco, 44, 83, 97, 136
Waggoner Ranch, 44, 46, 74, 77, 160
Walker, Robert "Daddy Warbucks," 159
Wall, 44
War and Weather (Powers), 99
Wardrip, Farylon Edward, 111
Wash, Wayne, 42, 90
Wayland Baptist University, 86
Weatherford, 7
Wells, Sheila Taylor, 116
West Texas A & M University, 134, 153
Westbrook Hotel, 119
White oil, 58
White, Hoolie, 86
Wichita Falls, v, vi, xi, 3, 11, 23, 46, 48, 57, 58, 69, 74, 81, 86, 89, 92, 95, 97, 106–107, 110–111, 156, 163
Wichita Falls Times Record News, 23,163, 166, 167
Wickett, 8
Williams, Clayton, 19, 50–51, 142
Williams, Mack, 119
Wills, Bob, 127, 130
Wilson, Carroll, 23
Windle, Janice Woods, 160
Winfrey, Oprah, 71, 73, 134
Wink, 44, 160, 163
Winters, 42, 86
Wood, Gordon, 39, 41–43, 87, 90

X

XIT Ranch, 1, 8, 27, 74, 77, 123

Y

Yates No. 30-A, 55

Z

Zephyr, 92